Financial
Intelligence

REVISED EDITION

Financial *Intelligence*

A Manager's Guide to Knowing What the Numbers Really Mean

KAREN BERMAN
JOE KNIGHT
with JOHN CASE

HARVARD BUSINESS REVIEW PRESS
BOSTON, MASSACHUSETTS

Printed in the United States of America
10 9 8

The web addresses referenced in this book were live and correct at the time of the book's publication but may be subject to change.

Library of Congress Cataloging-in-Publication Data

Berman, Karen, 1962–
Financial intelligence : a manager's guide to knowing what the numbers really mean / Karen Berman and Joe Knight ; with John Case. — 2nd ed., rev. and expanded.
p. cm.
ISBN 978-1-4221-4411-4 (alk. paper)
1. Financial statements. 2. Cash management. 3. Corporations—Finance.
I. Knight, Joe, 1963– II. Case, John, 1944– III. Title.
HG4028.B2B422 2013
658.15′11—dc23

2012039043

The paper used in this publication meets the minimum requirements of the American National Standard for Information Sciences—Permanence of Paper for Printed Library Materials, ANSI Z39.48-1992.

Karen dedicates this book to her husband, her daughter,
and her circle of family and friends.

Joe dedicates this book to his wife, Donielle, and to the
seven Js—Jacob, Jordan, Jewel, Jessica,
James, Jonah, and Joseph Christian (JC).

CONTENTS

PART THREE
THE BALANCE SHEET REVEALS THE MOST

PART FOUR
CASH IS KING

PART FIVE
RATIOS: LEARNING WHAT THE NUMBERS ARE REALLY TELLING YOU

PART SIX
HOW TO CALCULATE (AND REALLY UNDERSTAND) RETURN ON INVESTMENT

PART SEVEN
APPLIED FINANCIAL INTELLIGENCE: WORKING CAPITAL MANAGEMENT

PREFACE

WHAT IS FINANCIAL INTELLIGENCE?

We have worked with thousands of employees, managers, and leaders in companies all over the world, teaching them about the financial side of business. Our philosophy is that everyone in a company does better when they understand how financial success is measured and how they have an impact on the company's performance. Our term for that understanding is *financial intelligence*. Greater financial intelligence, we've learned, helps people feel more committed and involved. They understand better what they are a part of, what the organization is trying to achieve, and how they affect results. Trust increases, turnover decreases, and financial results improve.

We came to this philosophy by different routes. Karen took the academic path. Her PhD dissertation focused on the question of whether information sharing and financial understanding on the part of employees and managers positively affects a company's financial performance. (It does.) Karen went on to become a financial trainer and started an organization, the Business Literacy Institute, devoted to helping others learn about finance. Joe earned an MBA in finance, but most of his experience with financial training in organizations has been on the practical side. After stints at Ford Motor Company and several small companies, he joined a start-up business, Setpoint Systems and Setpoint Inc., which manufactures roller coasters and factory-automation equipment. As chief financial officer (CFO) and owner of Setpoint, he learned firsthand the importance of training engineers and other employees in how the business worked. In 2003 Joe joined Karen as co-owner of the Business Literacy Institute and since then has worked with dozens of companies, facilitating financial intelligence courses.

What do we mean by financial intelligence? It isn't some innate ability that you either have or don't have. Granted, some people are better at numbers than others, and a few legendary folks seem to have an intuitive grasp of finance that eludes the rest of us. But that's not what we're talking about here. For most businesspeople—ourselves included—financial intelligence is no more than a set of skills that can be learned. People who work in finance acquire these skills early on, and for the rest of their careers are able to talk with one another in a specialized language that can sound like Greek to the uninitiated. Most senior executives (not all) either come out of finance or pick up the skills during their rise to the top, just because it's tough to run a business unless you know what the financial folks are saying. Managers who don't work in finance, however, too often have been out of luck. They never picked up the skills, and so in some ways they've been relegated to the sidelines.

Fundamentally, financial intelligence boils down to four distinct skill sets, and when you finish the book, you should be competent in all of them. They are:

- *Understanding the foundation.* Managers who are financially intelligent understand the basics of financial measurement. They can read an income statement, a balance sheet, and a cash flow statement. They know the difference between profit and cash. They understand why the balance sheet balances. The numbers neither scare nor mystify them.

- *Understanding the art.* Finance and accounting are an art as well as a science. The two disciplines must try to quantify what can't always be quantified, and so must rely on rules, estimates, and assumptions. Financially intelligent managers are able to identify where the artful aspects of finance have been applied to the numbers, and they know how applying them differently might lead to different conclusions. They thus are prepared to question and challenge the numbers when appropriate.

- *Understanding analysis.* Once you have the foundation and an appreciation of the art of finance, you can use the information to analyze the numbers in greater depth. Financially intelligent managers don't shrink from ratios, return on investment (ROI) analysis, and the like. They use these analyses to inform their decisions, and they make better decisions for doing so.

- *Understanding the big picture.* Finally, although we teach finance, and although we think that everyone should understand the numbers side of business, we are equally firm in our belief that numbers can't and don't tell the whole story. A business's financial results must always be understood in context—that is, within the framework of the big picture. Factors such as the economy, the competitive environment, regulations, changing customer needs and expectations, and new technologies all affect how you should interpret numbers and make decisions.

But financial intelligence doesn't stop with book learning. Like most disciplines and skill sets, it must not only be learned, it must also be practiced and applied. On the practical side, we hope and expect the book will prepare you to take actions such as the following:

- *Speak the language.* Finance is the language of business. Whether you like it or not, the one thing every organization has in common is numbers and how those numbers are tabulated, analyzed, and reported. You need to *use* the language to be taken seriously and to communicate effectively. As with any new language, you can't expect to speak it fluently at first. Never mind—jump in and try something. You'll gain confidence as you go.

- *Ask questions.* We want you to look at financial reports and analysis with a questioning eye. It's not that we think anything is necessarily wrong with the numbers you see. We merely believe it is tremendously important to understand the what, why, and how of the numbers you are using to make decisions. Since every company is different, sometimes the only way to figure out all those parameters is to ask questions.

- *Use the information in your job.* After reading this book, you should know a lot. So use it! Use it to improve cash flow. Use it to analyze the next big project. Use it to assess your company's results. Your job will be more fun, and your impact on the company's performance will be greater. From our vantage point, we love to see employees, managers, and leaders who can see the link between financial results and their job. Suddenly, they seem to have a better idea of why they are carrying out a particular set of tasks.

Why This Second Edition?

Financial concepts don't change much from one year to the next, or even from one decade to the next. The fundamental concepts and ideas we discussed in the first edition of this book, published in 2006, are exactly the same in the current edition. But there are good reasons for presenting you with this revised and expanded version of the original text.

For one thing, the financial landscape has changed—and in a big way. Since the first edition of *Financial Intelligence* appeared, the world underwent a major crisis directly related to our topic. Suddenly more people than ever were talking about balance sheets, mark-to-market accounting, and liquidity ratios. The crisis also changed what was discussed inside companies: how the company was doing financially, how it could best be evaluated, and what financial issues managers and employees as individuals needed to consider.

To help facilitate these conversations, we added many new subjects, including the following:

- *A chapter on GAAP versus non-GAAP numbers.* Today, many companies are reporting both GAAP and non-GAAP results. (You can find out what GAAP and non-GAAP numbers are, and why they matter, in chapter 4.)

- *A chapter (chapter 25) that examines how the marketplace evaluates companies.* The financial crisis, like other bubbles and meltdowns, provided new insights into which measures are most (and least) helpful in understanding a company's financial performance.

- *Lots of additional information about return on investment (ROI),* including a section on the profitability index, a discussion of cost of capital, and an example of ROI analysis.

We also gathered up feedback from the thousands of people around the world who read the book, and from our clients who used it in their training classes. Thanks to that feedback, we have added several new concepts, such as contribution margin, the impact of exchange rates on profitability, and economic value added (EVA). We discuss bookings and backlog, deferred revenue, and return on net assets, or RONA. We think you'll find the book more useful as a result.

Finally, we added additional information about how to increase financial intelligence throughout your company. In our training business, we work with many companies, including dozens in the *Fortune* 500, who see this as a necessary part of employee, manager, and leader education.

So this book will support the development of your financial intelligence. We hope readers will find our experience and advice valuable. We hope it will enable you to achieve greater success, both personally and professionally. We hope it helps your company be more successful as well. But most of all, we think, after reading this book, you'll be just a bit more motivated, a bit more interested, and a bit more excited to understand a whole new aspect of business.

Part One

The Art of Finance (and Why It Matters)

1

You Can't Always Trust the Numbers

IF YOU READ THE NEWS REGULARLY, you have learned a good deal in recent years about all the wonderful ways people find to cook their companies' books. They record phantom sales. They hide expenses. They sequester some of their properties and debts in a mysterious place known as *off balance sheet.* Some of the techniques are pleasantly simple, like the software company a few years back that boosted revenues by shipping its customers empty cartons just before the end of a quarter. (The customers sent the cartons back, of course—but not until the following quarter.) Other techniques are complex to the point of near-incomprehensibility. (Remember Enron? It took years for accountants and prosecutors to sort out all of that ill-fated company's spurious transactions.) As long as there are liars and thieves on this earth, some of them will no doubt find ways to commit fraud and embezzlement.

But maybe you have also noticed something else about the arcane world of finance; namely, that many companies find perfectly legal ways to make their books look better than they otherwise would. Granted, these legitimate tools aren't quite as powerful as outright fraud: they can't make a bankrupt company look like a profitable one, at least not for long. But it's amazing what they *can* do. For example, a little technique called a *one-time charge* allows a company to take a whole bunch of bad news and cram it into one quarter's financial results, so that future quarters will look better. Alternatively, some shuffling of expenses from one category into another can pretty up a company's quarterly earnings picture and boost its stock price. A while ago, the *Wall Street Journal* ran a front-page story on how companies fatten their bottom lines by reducing retirees' benefit accruals—even though they may not spend a nickel less on those benefits.

Anybody who isn't a financial professional is likely to greet such maneuvers with a certain amount of mystification. Everything else in business—marketing, research and development, human resource management, strategy formulation, and so on—is obviously subjective, a matter dependent on experience and judgment as well as data. But finance? Accounting? Surely, the numbers produced by these departments are objective, black and white, indisputable. Surely, a company sold what it sold, spent what it spent, earned what it earned. Even where fraud is concerned, unless a company really does ship empty boxes, how can its executives so easily make things look so different than they really are? And short of fraud, how can they so easily manipulate the business's bottom line?

THE ART OF FINANCE

The fact is, accounting and finance, like all those other business disciplines, really are as much art as they are science. You might call this the CFO's or the controller's hidden secret, except that it isn't really a secret, it's a widely acknowledged truth that everyone in finance knows. Trouble is, the rest of us tend to forget it. We think that if a number shows up on the financial statements or the finance department's reports to management, it must accurately represent reality.

In fact, of course, that can't always be true, if only because even the numbers jockeys can't know everything. They can't know exactly what everyone in the company does every day, so they don't know exactly how to allocate costs. They can't know exactly how long a piece of equipment will last, so they don't know how much of its original cost to record in any given year. *The art of accounting and finance is the art of using limited data to come as close as possible to an accurate description of how well a company is performing*. Accounting and finance are not reality, they are a reflection of reality, and the accuracy of that reflection depends on the ability of accountants and finance professionals to make reasonable assumptions and to calculate reasonable estimates.

It's a tough job. Sometimes they have to quantify what can't easily be quantified. Sometimes they have to make difficult judgments about how to categorize a given item. None of these complications necessarily means that the accountants and financial folks are trying to cook the books or that they are incompetent. The complications arise because they must make educated guesses relating to the numbers side of the business all day long.

The result of these assumptions and estimates is, typically, a bias in the numbers. Please don't get the idea that by using the word *bias* we are impugning anybody's integrity. (Some of our best friends are accountants—no, really—and one of us, Joe, actually carries the title *CFO* on his business card.) Where financial results are concerned, *bias* means only that the numbers might be skewed in one direction or another, depending on the background or experience of the people who compiled and interpreted them. It means only that accountants and finance professionals have used certain assumptions and estimates rather than others when they put their reports together. Enabling you to understand this bias, to correct for it where necessary, and even to use it to your own (and your company's) advantage is one objective of this book. To understand it, you must know what questions to ask. Armed with the information you gather, you can make informed, well-considered decisions.

Box Definitions

We want to make finance as easy as possible. Most finance books make us flip back and forth between the page we're on and the glossary to learn the definition of a word we don't know. By the time we find it and get back to our page, we've lost our train of thought. So here, we are going to give you the definitions right where you need them, next to the first time we use the word.

JUDGMENT CALLS

For example, let's look at one of the variables that is frequently estimated—one that you wouldn't think needed to be estimated at all. *Revenue* or *sales* refers to the value of what a company sold to its customers during a given period. You'd think that would be an easy matter to determine. But the question is, When should revenue be recorded (or "recognized," as accountants like to say)? Here are some possibilities:

- When a contract is signed
- When the product or service is delivered
- When the invoice is sent out
- When the bill is paid

If you said, "When the product or service is delivered," you're correct. As we'll see in chapter 7, that's the fundamental rule that determines when a sale should show up on the income statement. Still, the rule isn't simple. Implementing it requires making a number of assumptions, and in fact the whole question of "When is a sale a sale?" is a hot topic in many fraud cases. According to a 2007 study by the Deloitte Forensic Center, 41 percent of fraud cases pursued by the Securities and Exchange Commission between 2000 and 2006 involved revenue recognition.[1]

Income Statement

The income statement shows revenues, expenses, and profit for a period of time, such as a month, quarter, or year. It's also called a profit and loss statement, P&L, statement of earnings, or statement of operations. Sometimes the word *consolidated* is thrown in front of those phrases, but it's still just an income statement. The bottom line of the income statement is *net profit*, also known as net income or net earnings.

Imagine, for instance, that a company sells a customer a copying machine, complete with a maintenance contract, all wrapped up in one financial package. Suppose the machine is delivered in October, but the maintenance contract is good for the following twelve months. Now: How much of the initial purchase price should be recorded on the books for October? After all, the company hasn't yet delivered all the services that it is responsible for during the year. Accountants can make estimates of the value of those services, of course, and adjust the revenue accordingly. But this requires a big judgment call.

Nor is this example merely hypothetical. Witness Xerox, which several years ago played the revenue-recognition game on such a massive scale that it was later found to have improperly recognized a whopping $6 billion of sales. The issue? Xerox was selling equipment on four-year leases, including service and maintenance. So how much of the price covered the cost of the equipment, and how much was for the subsequent services? Fearful that the company's sagging profits would cause its stock price to plummet, Xerox's executives at the time decided to book ever-increasing percentages of the anticipated revenues—along with the associated profits—up front. Before long, nearly all the revenue on these contracts was being recognized at the time of the sale.

Xerox had clearly lost its way and was trying to use accounting to cover up its business failings. But you can see the point here: there's plenty of room, short of outright book-cooking, to make the numbers look one way or another.

A second example of the artful work of finance—and another one that often plays a role in financial scandals—is determining whether a given

Operating Expenses

Operating expenses are the costs required to keep the business going from day to day. They include salaries, benefits, and insurance costs, among a host of other items. Operating expenses are listed on the income statement and are subtracted from revenue to determine profit.

cost is a capital expenditure or an operating expense. (The Deloitte study notes that this issue accounted for 11 percent of fraud cases between 2000 and 2006.) We'll get to all the details later; for the moment, all you need to know is that an operating expense reduces the bottom line immediately, and a capital expenditure spreads the hit out over several accounting periods. You can see the temptation here: *Wait. You mean if we take all those office supply purchases and call them "capital expenditures," we can increase our profit accordingly?* This is the kind of thinking that got WorldCom—the big telecommunications company that went bankrupt in 2002—into so much trouble (see the part 3 toolbox for details). To prevent such temptation, both the accounting profession and individual companies have rules about what must be classified where. But the rules leave a good deal up to individual judgment and discretion. Again, those judgments can affect a company's profit, and hence its stock price, dramatically.

Now, we are writing this book primarily for people in companies, not for investors. So why should these readers worry about any of this? The reason, of course, is that they use numbers to make decisions. You yourself make judgments about budgets, capital expenditures, staffing, and a dozen other matters—or your boss does—based on an assessment of the company's or your business unit's financial situation. If you aren't aware of the assumptions and estimates that underlie the numbers and how those assumptions and estimates affect the numbers in one direction or another, your decisions may be faulty. Financial intelligence means understanding where the numbers are "hard"—well supported and relatively uncontroversial—and

Capital Expenditures

A capital expenditure is the purchase of an item that's considered a long-term investment, such as computer systems and equipment. Most companies follow the rule that any purchase over a certain dollar amount counts as a capital expenditure, while anything less is an operating expense. Operating expenses show up on the income statement, and thus reduce profit. Capital expenditures show up on the balance sheet; only the *depreciation* of a piece of capital equipment appears on the income statement. More on this in chapters 5 and 11.

where they are "soft"—that is, highly dependent on judgment calls. What's more, outside investors, bankers, vendors, customers, and others will be using your company's numbers as a basis for their own decisions. If you don't have a good working understanding of the financial statements and know what they're looking at or why, you are at their mercy.

2

Spotting Assumptions, Estimates, and Biases

SO LET'S PLUNGE A LITTLE DEEPER into this element of financial intelligence—understanding the "artistic" aspects of finance. Even though you're just at the beginning of the book, this will give you a valuable perspective on the concepts and practices that you'll learn later on. We'll look at three examples and ask some simple but critical questions:

- What were the assumptions in this number?
- Are there any estimates in the numbers?
- What is the bias those assumptions and estimates lead to?
- What are the implications?

The examples we'll look at are accruals, depreciation, and valuation. If these words sound like part of that strange language the financial folks speak, don't worry. You'll be surprised how quickly you can pick up enough to get around.

ACCRUALS AND ALLOCATIONS: LOTS OF ASSUMPTIONS AND ESTIMATES

At a certain time every month, you know that your company's controller is busy "closing the books." Here, too, is a financial puzzle: Why on earth does it take as long as it does? If you haven't worked in finance, you might think it could take a day to add up all the end-of-the-month figures. But two or three *weeks*?

Well, one step that takes a lot of time is figuring out all the *accruals* and *allocations*. There's no need to understand the details now—we'll get to that in chapters 11 and 12. For the moment, read the definitions in the boxes and focus on the fact that the accountants use accruals and allocations to try to create an accurate picture of the business for the month. After all, it doesn't help anybody if the financial reports don't tell us how much it cost us to produce the products and services we sold last month. That is what the controller's staff is trying so hard to do, and that is one reason why it takes as long as it does.

Determining accruals and allocations nearly always entails making assumptions and estimates. Take your salary as an example. Say that you worked in June on a new product line and that the new line was introduced in July. Now the accountant determining the allocations has to estimate how much of your salary should be matched to the product cost (because you spent much of your time on those initial products) and how much should be charged to development costs (because you also worked on the original development of the product). She must also decide how to accrue for June versus July. Depending on how she answers questions

Accruals

An accrual is the portion of a revenue or expense item that is recorded in a particular time span. Product development costs, for instance, are likely to be spread out over several accounting periods, and so a portion of the total cost will be *accrued* each month. The purpose of accruals is to match costs to revenues in a given time period as accurately as possible.

Allocations

Allocations are apportionments of costs to different departments or activities within a company. For instance, overhead costs such as the CEO's salary are often allocated to the company's operating units.

such as these, she can dramatically change the appearance of the income statement. Product cost goes into cost of goods sold. If product costs go up, gross profit goes down—and gross profit is a key measure for assessing product profitability. Development costs, however, go into R&D, which is included in the operating expense section of the income statement and doesn't affect gross profit at all.

So let's say the accountant determined that all of your salary should go into the development cost in June, rather than the product cost in July. Her assumption is that your work wasn't directly related to the manufacturing of the product and therefore shouldn't be categorized as product cost. But there's a twofold bias that results:

- First, development costs are larger than they otherwise would be. An executive who analyzes those costs later on may decide that product development is too expensive and that the company shouldn't take that risk again. If that's what happens, the company might do less product development, thereby jeopardizing its future.
- Second, the product cost is smaller than it otherwise would be. That, in turn, will affect key decisions such as pricing and hiring. Maybe the product will be priced too low. Maybe more people will be hired to put out what looks like a profitable product—even though the profit reflects some dubious assumptions.

Of course, any individual's salary won't make much of a difference in most companies. But the assumptions that govern one person are likely to be applied across the board. To paraphrase a familiar saying in Washington, DC, a salary here and a salary there and pretty soon you're talking real money. At any rate, this case is simple enough that you can easily see the answers to the questions we posed earlier. The assumptions in the numbers? Your time was spent in development and didn't really have much to do with the production of the product that was sold in July. The estimates? How your salary should be split, if at all, between development and product cost. The bias? Higher development costs and lower product costs. And the implications? Concern about the high cost of development; product pricing that may be too low.

Whoever said there is no poignancy or subtlety in finance? The accountant and finance professional labor to give the most accurate picture possible of the company's performance. All the while they know that they will never, ever capture the exact numbers.

DISCRETION ABOUT DEPRECIATION

A second example is the use of *depreciation*. The notion of depreciation isn't complicated. Say a company buys some expensive machinery or vehicles that it expects to use for several years. Accountants think about such an event like this: rather than subtract the entire cost from one month's revenues—perhaps plunging the company or business unit into the red for that month—we should spread the cost out over the equipment's useful life. If we think a machine will last three years, for instance, we can record ("depreciate") one-third of the cost per year, or one-thirty-sixth per month, using a simple method of depreciation. That's a better way of estimating the company's true costs in any given month or year than if we

Depreciation

Depreciation is the method accountants use to allocate the cost of equipment and other assets to the total cost of products and services as shown on the income statement. It is based on the same idea as accruals: we want to match as closely as possible the costs of our products and services with what was sold. Most capital investments other than land are depreciated. Accountants attempt to spread the cost of the expenditure over the useful life of the item. There's more about depreciation in parts 2 and 3.

recorded it all at once. Furthermore, it better matches the expenses of the equipment to the revenue that it is used to generate—an important idea that we will explore at length in chapter 5.

The theory makes perfect sense. In practice, however, accountants have a good deal of discretion as to exactly how a piece of equipment is depreciated. And that discretion can have a considerable impact. Take the airline industry. Some years back, airlines realized that their planes were lasting longer than anticipated. So the industry's accountants changed their depreciation schedules to reflect that longer life. As a result, they subtracted less depreciation from revenue each month. And guess what? The industry's profits rose significantly, reflecting the fact that the airlines wouldn't have to be buying planes as soon as they had thought. But note that the accountants had to assume that they could predict how long a plane would be useful. On that judgment—and a judgment it is—hung the resulting upward bias in the profit numbers. On that judgment, too, hung all the implications: investors deciding to buy more stock, airline executives figuring they could afford to give out better raises, and so on.

THE MANY METHODS OF VALUATION

A final example of the art of finance has to do with the *valuation* of a company—that is, figuring out how much a company is worth. Publicly traded companies, of course, are valued every day by the stock market. They are worth whatever their stock price is times the number of shares outstanding, a figure known as their *market capitalization*, or just market cap. But even that doesn't necessarily capture their value in certain circumstances. A competitor bent on takeover, for instance, might decide to pay a premium for the company's shares, because the target company is worth more to that competitor than it is on the open market. And of course, the millions of companies that are privately held aren't valued at all on the market. When they are bought or sold, the buyers and sellers must rely on other methods of valuation.

Talk about the art of finance: much of the art here lies in choosing the valuation method. Different methods produce different results—which, of course, means that each method injects a bias into the numbers.

Suppose, for example, your company proposes to acquire a closely held manufacturer of industrial valves. It's a good fit with your business—it's a "strategic" acquisition—but how much should your company pay? Well, you could look at the valve company's earnings (another word for profits), then go to the public markets and see how the market values similar companies in relation to their earnings. (This is known as the *price-to-earnings ratio method.*) Or you could look at how much cash the valve company generates each year, and figure that you are, in effect, buying that stream of cash. Then you would use some interest rate to determine what that stream of future cash is worth today. (This is the *discounted cash flow method.*) Alternatively, you could simply look at the company's assets—its plant, equipment, inventory, and so on, along with intangibles such as its reputation and customer list—and make estimates about what those assets are worth (the *asset valuation method*).

Needless to say, each method entails a whole passel of assumptions and estimates. The price-to-earnings method, for example, assumes that the stock market is somehow rational and that the prices it sets are therefore accurate. But of course the market isn't wholly rational; if the market is high, the value of your target company will be higher than when the market is low. And besides, that "earnings" number, as we'll see in part 2, is *itself* an estimate. So maybe, you might think, we should use the discounted cash flow method. The question with this method is, What is the right interest or "discount" rate to use when we're calculating the value of that stream of cash? Depending on how we set it, the price could vary enormously. And of course, the asset valuation method itself is merely a collection of guesses as to what each asset might be worth.

As if these uncertainties weren't enough, think back to that delightful, outrageous, nervous-making period, known as the *dot-com boom*, at the end of the twentieth century. Ambitious young Internet companies were springing up all over, fed and watered by a torrent of enthusiastic venture capital. But when investors such as venture capitalists (VCs) put their money into something, they like to know what their investment—and hence what the company—is worth. When a company is just starting up, that's tough to know. Earnings? Zero. Operating cash flow? Also zero. Assets? Negligible. In ordinary times, that's one reason VCs shy away from early-stage investments. But in the dot-com era, they were throwing caution to the winds and so were relying on what we can only call unusual methods of valuation. They looked at the number of engineers on a company's payroll. They counted the number of hits ("eyeballs") a company got every month on its website. One energetic young CEO of our acquaintance raised millions of dollars based almost entirely on the fact that he had hired a large staff of software engineers. Unfortunately, we observed a "For Lease" sign in front of this company's office less than a year later.

The dot-com methods of valuation look foolish now, even though back then they didn't seem so bad, given how little we knew about what the future held. But the other methods described earlier are all reasonable. Trouble is, each has a bias that leads to different results. And the implications are far-reaching. Companies are bought and sold on the basis of these valuations. They get loans based on them. If you hold stock in your company, the value of that stock is dependent on an appropriate valuation. It seems reasonable to us that your financial intelligence should include an understanding of how those numbers are calculated.

3

Why Increase Your Financial Intelligence?

SO FAR OUR DISCUSSION HAS BEEN PRETTY ABSTRACT. We have been introducing you to the art of finance and explaining why understanding it is an essential ingredient of financial intelligence. Now let's revisit the issue we posed in the preface: the benefits of financial intelligence. With a little art-of-finance discussion under your belt, you can understand in greater depth what this book can teach you and what you will gain from reading it.

For starters, we want to emphasize that this book is different from other finance books. It doesn't presuppose any financial knowledge. But neither is it another version of *Accounting for Dummies*. We will never mention debits and credits. We won't ever refer to the general ledger or trial balances. This book is about financial intelligence, or, as the subtitle says, *knowing what the numbers really mean*. It's written not for would-be accountants but for people in organizations—leaders, managers, employees—who need to understand what is happening in their company from a financial perspective and who can use that information to work and manage more effectively. In it, you'll learn how to decipher the financial statements, how to identify potential biases in the numbers, and how to use the information in the statements to do your job better. You'll learn how to calculate ratios. You'll learn about return on investment (ROI) and working capital management, two concepts that you can use to improve your decision making and impact on the organization. In short, you will boost your financial intelligence.

If you boost your financial intelligence, moreover, you will very likely stand out from the crowd. Not long ago, we conducted a national study, giving a twenty-one-question finance exam to a representative sample of nonfinancial managers in the United States. The questions were all based on concepts that any company executive or junior finance person would know. Unfortunately, the managers scored an average of only 38 percent—a failing grade by any standard. To judge by their answers, a majority were unable to distinguish profit from cash. Many didn't know the difference between an income statement and a balance sheet. About 70 percent couldn't pick the correct definition of free cash flow, now the measure of choice for many Wall Street investors.[1] By the time you finish this book, you will know all that material, and a good deal more besides. That's what we mean by standing out from the crowd.

THE BENEFITS OF FINANCIAL INTELLIGENCE

But it isn't just a matter of scoring well on a test; financial intelligence brings with it a host of practical benefits. Here's a short list of the advantages you'll gain.

Increased Ability to Critically Evaluate Your Company

Do you really know if your employer has enough cash to make payroll? Do you know how profitable the products or services you work on really are? When it comes to capital-expenditure proposals, is the ROI analysis based on solid data? Boost your financial intelligence, and you'll gain more insight into questions like these. Or maybe you've had nightmares in which you worked at AIG, Lehman Brothers, or maybe Washington Mutual. Many of the people at those companies had no inkling of their precarious situation.

Suppose, for instance, you worked at the big telecommunications company WorldCom (later known as MCI) during the late 1990s. WorldCom's strategy was to grow through acquisition. Trouble was, the company wasn't generating enough cash for the acquisitions it wanted to make. So it used stock as its currency and paid for the companies it acquired partly with

WorldCom shares. That meant it absolutely had to keep its share price high; otherwise, the acquisitions would be too expensive. And if you want to keep your share price high, you'd better keep your profits high. Moreover, WorldCom paid for the acquisitions through borrowing. A company doing a lot of borrowing also has to keep its profits up; otherwise, the banks will stop lending it money. So on two fronts, WorldCom was under severe pressure to report high profits.

That, of course, was the source of the fraud that was ultimately uncovered. The company artificially boosted profits "with a variety of accounting tricks, including understating expenses and treating operating costs as capital expenditures," as *Business Week* summarized the Justice Department's indictment.[2] When everybody learned that WorldCom was not as profitable as it had claimed to be, the house of cards came tumbling down. But even if there hadn't been fraud, WorldCom's ability to generate cash was out of step with its growth-by-acquisitions strategy. It could live on borrowing and stock for a while, but not forever.

Or look at Tyco International. For a while, Tyco was another big acquirer of companies. In fact, it bought some six hundred companies in just two years, or more than one every working day. With all those acquisitions, the goodwill number on Tyco's balance sheet grew to the point where bankers began to get nervous. Bankers and investors don't like to see too much goodwill on a balance sheet; they prefer assets that you can touch (and in a pinch, sell off). So when word spread that there might be some

Goodwill

Goodwill comes into play when one company acquires another company. It is the difference between the net assets acquired (that is, the fair market value of the assets less the assumed liabilities) and the amount of money the acquiring company pays for them. For example, if a company's net assets are valued at $1 million and the acquirer pays $3 million, then goodwill of $2 million goes onto the acquirer's balance sheet. That $2 million reflects all the value that is not reflected in the acquiree's tangible assets—for example, its name, reputation, and so on.

Balance Sheet

The balance sheet reflects the assets, liabilities, and owners' equity at a point in time. In other words, it shows, on a specific day, what the company owned, what it owed, and how much it was worth. The balance sheet is called such because it balances—assets always must equal liabilities plus owners' equity. A financially savvy manager knows that all the financial statements ultimately flow to the balance sheet. We'll explain all these notions in part 3.

accounting irregularities at Tyco, the bankers effectively shut the company off from further acquisitions immediately. Today Tyco is focusing on organic growth and operational excellence rather than on acquisitions; its financial picture matches its strategy.

Now, we're not arguing that every financially intelligent manager would have been able to spot AIG's or Tyco's precarious situation. Plenty of seemingly savvy Wall Street types were fooled by the two companies. Still, a little more knowledge will give you the tools to watch trends at your company and understand more of the stories behind the numbers. While you might not have all of the answers, you should know what questions to ask when you don't. It's always worth your while to assess your company's performance and prospects. You'll learn to gauge how it's doing and to figure out how you can best support those goals and be successful yourself.

Better Understanding of the Bias in the Numbers

We've already discussed the bias that is built into many numbers. But so what? What will understanding the bias do for you? One very big thing: it will give you the knowledge and the confidence—the financial intelligence—to *question the data provided by your finance and accounting department*. You will be able to identify the hard data, the assumptions, and the estimates. You will know—and others will, too—when your decisions and actions are on solid ground.

Let's say you work in operations, and you are proposing the purchase of some new equipment. Your boss says he'll listen, but he wants you to justify the purchase. That means digging up data from finance, including cash flow analysis for the machine, working capital requirements, and depreciation schedules. All these numbers—surprise!—are based on assumptions and estimates. If you know what they are, you can examine them to see if they make sense. If they don't, you can change the assumptions, modify the estimates, and put together an analysis that is realistic and that (hopefully) supports your proposal. Joe, for example, likes to tell audiences that a financially savvy engineer could easily come up with an analysis showing how his company should buy him a $5,000 CAD/CAM machine, complete with the latest software. The engineer would assume that he could save an hour a day because of the new computer's features and processing speed; he would calculate the value of an hour per day of his time over a year; and—presto!—he would show that buying the machine is a no-brainer. A financially intelligent boss, however, would take a look at those assumptions and posit some alternatives, such as that the engineer might actually *lose* an hour a day of work while he played with all the cool features on the new machine.

It's amazing, in fact, how easily a financially knowledgeable manager can change the terms of discussion so that better decisions get made. When he worked for Ford Motor Company, Joe had an experience that underlined just that lesson. He and several other finance folks were presenting financial results to a senior marketing director. After they sat down, the director looked straight at them and said, "Before I open these finance reports, I need to know . . . for how long and at what temperature?" Joe and the others had no idea what he was talking about. Then the light went on and Joe replied, "Yes, sir, they were in for two hours at 350°." The director said, "OK, now that I know how long you cooked 'em, let's begin." He was telling the finance people that he knew there were assumptions and estimates in the numbers and that he was going to ask questions. When he asked in the meeting how solid a given number was, the financial people were comfortable explaining where the number came from and the assumptions, if any, they had to make. The director could then take the numbers and use them to make decisions he felt comfortable with.

Absent such knowledge, what happens? Simple: the people from accounting and finance control the decisions. We use the word *control* because when decisions are based on numbers, and when the numbers are based on accountants' assumptions and estimates, then the accountants and finance folks have effective control (even if they aren't trying to control anything). That's why you need to know what questions to ask.

The Ability to Use Numbers and Financial Tools to Make and Analyze Decisions

What is the ROI of that project? Why can't we spend money when our company is profitable? Why do I have to focus on accounts receivable when I am not in the accounting department? You ask yourself these and other questions every day (or someone else asks them—and assumes you know the answers!). You are expected to use financial knowledge to make decisions, to direct your subordinates, and to plan the future of your department or company. We will show you how to do this, give you examples, and discuss what to do with the results. In the process, we'll try to use as little financial jargon as possible.

For example, let's look at why the finance department might tell you not to spend any money, even though the company is profitable.

We'll start with the basic fact that cash and profit are different. In chapter 16 we'll explain why, but right now let's just focus on the basics. Profit is based on revenue. Revenue, remember, is recognized when a product or service is delivered, not when the bill is paid. So the top line of the income statement, the line from which we subtract expenses to determine profit, is often no more than a promise. Customers have not paid yet, so the revenue number does not reflect real money and neither does the profit line at the bottom. If everything goes well, the company will eventually collect its receivables and will have cash corresponding to that profit. In the meantime, it doesn't.

Now suppose you're working for a fast-growing business services company. The company is selling a lot of services at a good price, so its revenues and profits are high. It is hiring people as fast as it can, and of course it has to pay them as soon as they come on board. But all the profit that these people are earning won't turn into cash until thirty days or maybe sixty days after it is billed out! That's one reason why even the CFO of a highly profitable company may sometimes say, don't spend any money right now because cash is tight.

Cash

Cash as presented on the balance sheet means the money a company has in the bank, plus anything else (like stocks and bonds) that can readily be turned into cash. Really, it's that simple. Later we'll discuss measures of cash flow. For now, just know that when companies talk about cash, it really is the cold, hard stuff.

Although this book focuses on increasing your financial intelligence in business, you can also apply what you'll learn in your personal life. Consider your decisions to purchase a house, a car, or a boat. The knowledge you'll gain can apply to those decisions as well. Or consider how you plan for the future and decide how to invest. This book is not about investing, but it is about understanding company financials, which will help you analyze possible investment opportunities.

HOW IT BENEFITS A COMPANY

Our day job is teaching financial literacy, thereby (we hope) increasing the financial intelligence of the leaders, managers, and employees who are our students. So naturally, we think it's an important subject for our students to learn. But what we have also seen in our work is how increasing financial intelligence benefits companies. Again, here is a short list of advantages.

Strength and Balance Throughout the Organization

Do the finance folks dominate decisions? They shouldn't. The strength of their department should be balanced by the strength of operations, of marketing, of human resources, of customer service, of information technology, and so on. If managers in those other departments are not financially savvy, if they don't understand how financial results are measured and how to use those results to critically evaluate the company, then accounting and finance necessarily have the upper hand. The bias they inject into the numbers affects and can even determine decision making.

Better Decisions

Managers routinely incorporate what they know about the marketplace, the competition, the customers, and so on into their decisions. When they also incorporate financial analysis, their decisions are better. We are not big believers in making decisions solely on the basis of the numbers. But we do think that ignoring what the numbers tell you is pretty silly. Good financial analysis gives managers a window into the future and helps them make smarter, more informed choices.

Greater Alignment

Imagine the power in your organization if *everyone* understood the financial side of the business. Everyone might actually work in alignment with the strategy and goals. Everyone might work as a team to achieve healthy profitability and cash flow. Everyone might communicate in the language of business instead of jockeying for position through office politics. Wow.

ROADBLOCKS TO FINANCIAL SAVVY

We have worked with enough people and companies to know that while the results everyone wants might be great, they aren't so easy to attain. In fact, we run into several predictable obstacles, both personal and organizational.

One obstacle might be that you hate math, fear math, and don't want to do math. Well, join the club. It might surprise you to know that, for the most part, finance involves addition and subtraction. When finance people get really fancy, they multiply and divide. We never have to take the second derivative of a function or determine the area under a curve (sorry, engineers). So have no fear: the math is easy. And calculators are cheap. You don't need to be a rocket scientist to be financially intelligent.

A second possible obstacle: the accounting and finance departments hold on tightly to all the information. Are your finance folks stuck in the old approach to their field—keepers and controllers of the numbers, reluctant participants in the communication process? Are they focused on control and compliance? If so, that means you may have a difficult time getting access to data. But you can still use what you learn to talk about the numbers at your management meetings. You can use the tools to help you make a decision, or to ask questions about the assumptions and estimates in the numbers. In fact, you'll probably surprise and maybe delight your accountants and finance people. We love to see it when it happens.

A third possibility is that your boss doesn't want you to question the numbers. If that's the case, he himself may not be comfortable with financials. He probably doesn't know about the assumptions, estimates, and resulting bias. Your boss is a victim of the numbers! Our advice is to keep going; eventually, bosses usually see the benefit to themselves, their departments, and their companies. You can help them along. The more people who do so, the more financially intelligent the entire organization will be. You can also begin to take some risks. Your financial knowledge will give you newfound power, and you can ask some probing questions.

A fourth possibility: you don't have time. Just give us the time it takes you to read this book. If you fly for business, take it with you on a trip or two. In just a few hours, you will become a lot more knowledgeable about finance than you have ever been in the past. Alternatively, keep it someplace handy. The chapters are deliberately short, and you can read one whenever you have a few spare moments. Incidentally, we've included some stories about the fancy financial shenanigans pulled by some of the corporate villains in the 1990s and 2000s just to make it a little more entertaining—and to show you how slippery some of these slopes can be. We don't mean to imply that every company is like them; on the contrary, most are doing their best to present a fair and honest picture of their performance. But it's always fun to read about the bad guys.

So don't let these obstacles get in your way. Read the book, and learn what you can about your own company. Soon you will have a healthy appreciation of the art of finance, and you will increase your financial intelligence. You won't magically acquire an MBA in finance, but you will be an appreciative consumer of the numbers, someone who's capable of understanding and assessing what the financial folks are showing you and asking them appropriate questions. The numbers will no longer scare you. It won't take long, it's relatively painless, and it will mean a lot to your career.

4

The Rules Accountants Follow—and Why You Don't Always Have To

WE DON'T PLAN TO INCLUDE more than a smattering of accounting procedures in this book. But we do think it's a good idea to have a broad grasp of the rules accountants are supposed to follow. That will help you understand why they choose to rely on certain estimates and assumptions and not others. Besides, some companies prepare financials for their own use that do *not* follow these rules—and those documents can be valuable, too.

So let's begin at the beginning. Accountants in the United States rely on a set of guidelines known as Generally Accepted Accounting Principles, or GAAP (pronounced *gap*) for short. GAAP includes all the rules, standards, and procedures that companies use when preparing their financial statements. GAAP rules are established and administered by the Financial Accounting Standards Board, or FASB (pronounced *fasby*) and the American Institute of Certified Public Accountants (AICPA, pronounced *A-I-C-P-A*). The Securities and Exchange Commission requires publicly traded companies to adhere to GAAP standards. Most privately held companies, nonprofits, and governments also use GAAP. Strictly speaking, we should use the phrase US GAAP, because these rules apply only to American companies. (We'll have more to say in a moment on international standards.)

If you were to lay out all the GAAP pronouncements on paper, page by page, some people estimate they would run to more than 100,000 pages. Accountants who use GAAP to prepare financial statements typically are experts in one area of the rules, such as depreciation. We haven't yet met anyone who has read and is an expert on the entire code.

RULES THAT AREN'T REALLY RULES

The purpose of GAAP is to make financial information useful to investors, creditors, and others who make decisions based on a company's financial reporting. GAAP reporting is also supposed to provide helpful information to company executives and managers—information that will lead to improving the business's performance and will be useful in maintaining company records.

But GAAP rules are not what most people might think of as "rules." They don't take the form of imperatives, such as "Count this expense exactly this way" or "Count this revenue exactly that way." They are guidelines and principles, and so are open to interpretation and judgment calls. A company's accountants must figure out how a given principle applies to their business. This is a big part of the art of finance. Remember, the accountants and finance professionals are attempting to create a picture of reality through the numbers. It will never be exact or perfect, but it does need to be tailored to their own individual situation. GAAP allows that.

If you look at the footnotes of public company's financials, you'll often see that some of the notes explain how the company's accountants interpreted GAAP guidelines. For example, one of the footnotes on Ford's 2010 financials reads as follows:

> *We are required by US GAAP to aggregate the assets and liabilities of all held-for-sale disposal groups on the balance sheet for the period in which the disposal group is held for sale. To provide comparative balance sheets, we also aggregate the assets and liabilities for significant held-for-sale disposal groups on the prior-period balance sheet.*

Wow. How's that for financial jargon? But at least the accountants are explaining their GAAP-related practices in terms other financial professionals can understand.

Sometimes it happens that the accountants have to restate their financials. Maybe they identified new information, or perhaps they discovered an error. Maybe the GAAP rules changed. Apple, for example, restated its 2009 results, as announced in a press release on January 5, 2010:

> ****Retrospective Adoption of Amended Accounting Standards***
>
> *The new accounting principles result in the Company's recognition of substantially all of the revenue and product cost for iPhone and Apple TV when those products are delivered to customers. Under historical accounting principles, the Company was required to account for sales of both iPhone and Apple TV using subscription accounting because the Company indicated it might from time to time provide future unspecified software upgrades and features for those products free of charge. Under subscription accounting, revenue and associated product cost of sales for iPhone and Apple TV were deferred at the time of sale and recognized on a straight-line basis over each product's estimated economic life. This resulted in the deferral of significant amounts of revenue and cost of sales related to iPhone and Apple TV.*
>
> *Because Apple began selling both iPhone and Apple TV in fiscal 2007, the Company retrospectively adopted the new accounting principles as if the new accounting principles had been applied in all prior periods . . .*

Again, this is more than any nonfinancial person probably wants to know. But if you're an investor trying to assess Apple's performance from year to year, you need to understand exactly why and how the company restated its financials. Otherwise you're comparing pears to peaches.

WHY GAAP MATTERS

A common set of accounting rules provides several benefits. It gives investors and others a reliable way to compare financial results between companies, between industries, and from one year to another. If every company assembled its financials differently, using whatever rules it felt were appropriate, the results would be like the United Nations without translators. Nobody could understand anybody else, and nobody could compare Ford with GM or Microsoft with Apple. You wouldn't know, for example, if the companies counted sales and costs the same way, and you could never really know which was more profitable.

GAAP also attempts to ensure that everything is on the up-and-up. To be sure, people are always figuring out ways to get around the rules. And Warren Buffett, the legendary investor, is famous for the warnings he has issued, such as this classic one from his 1988 letter to his shareholders:

> *There are managers who actively use GAAP to deceive and defraud. They know that many investors and creditors accept GAAP results as gospel. So these charlatans interpret the rules "imaginatively" and record business transactions in ways that technically comply with GAAP but actually display an economic illusion to the world. As long as investors—including supposedly sophisticated institutions—place fancy valuations on reported "earnings" that march steadily upward, you can be sure that some managers and promoters will exploit GAAP to produce such numbers, no matter what the truth may be. Over the years, [my partner] Charlie Munger and I have observed many accounting-based frauds of staggering size. Few of the perpetrators have been punished; many have not even been [c]ensured. It has been far safer to steal large sums with a pen than small sums with a gun.*

Despite such malfeasance, GAAP provides a touchstone, a body of guidelines that most companies, if not all, follow closely. FASB and the AICPA continually revise and update the rules to reflect new issues and concerns, so GAAP is a living entity that evolves with the times.

THE KEY PRINCIPLES

There are several principles that form the foundation of GAAP and GAAP-based financial statements. Knowing these principles will help you understand what can and cannot be found in the financials.

Monetary Units and Historical Cost

This principle states that all items in financial statements are expressed in monetary units, such as dollars, euros, or whatever. It also says that the price a company paid for an asset, which accountants call *historical cost*, is the basis for determining its value. (Assets are what a company owns.) We're getting into some art-of-finance issues here. For example, a building may be worth far more today than when it was built, yet its valuation on the books will be what it originally cost the company. However, companies do not typically value financial assets such as stocks and bonds at historical cost. The accountants are required to value financial assets at their current market value. This is known as *mark-to-market accounting*, and we discuss it in the toolbox following part 3.

You can see why the footnotes to the financial statements often come in handy. The footnotes tell you how assets are valued, and you may be able to see whether the company's assets might be worth more or less than indicated on the financials.

Conservatism

GAAP requires accountants to be *conservative*. No, we don't mean in their politics or their lifestyle, only in their accounting—although maybe that explains why the stereotypical accountant *is* conservative in other areas of life. Conservatism in accounting means, for example, that when a company expects a loss, the loss must show up in the financial statements as soon as it can be quantified—that is, as soon as the amounts involved are known. Accountants call this *recognizing* a loss.

It's the opposite with gains. When a company expects a gain, the accountants can't record it until they know for sure that the gain actually happened. Let's imagine, for instance, that a company makes a sale. Can the accountants put it in the books? Only, says GAAP, if they are satisfied that at least four conditions hold:

- *There is persuasive evidence that an arrangement exists.* This just means the company is confident that a sale really did happen.
- *Delivery has occurred or services have been rendered.* What was sold is somehow delivered to the customer.

- *The seller's price to the buyer is fixed or determinable.* The price must be known.
- *Collectability is reasonably assured.* You can't count it as a sale if you don't think you can collect.

In most cases, of course, all these conditions are easily met. Accountants have to make judgment calls only on the margins.

Consistency

GAAP offers guidelines rather than rules, so companies can make choices about the accounting methods and assumptions they use. Once a company selects a particular method or assumption, however, it should continue to use that method or assumption unless something in the business warrants a change. In other words, you can't alter your methods or assumptions every year without good reason. If the accountants decided on different assumptions every year, nobody could compare results year to year, and you as a manager wouldn't know what the numbers were really telling you. Then, too, companies might change methods and assumptions just to make the numbers look better each year.

Full Disclosure

Full disclosure relates to the previous guideline, consistency. If a company changes an accounting method or assumption and the change has a material impact (more on "material" in a minute), then it must disclose both the change and the financial effects of that change. You can see the logic. Those of us reading the reports need to know about changes and their impact to fully understand what the numbers mean. Companies take this requirement seriously. In the example below, Ford disclosed a change in its 2010 financials even though it did *not* have a material impact—an appropriately conservative approach.

> Transfers of Financial Assets. *During the first quarter of 2010, we adopted the new accounting standard related to transfers of financial assets. The standard requires greater transparency about transfers of financial assets and a company's continuing involvement in the transferred financial assets. The standard also removes the concept of a qualifying special-purpose*

entity from US GAAP and changes the requirements for derecognizing financial assets. The new accounting standard did not have a material impact on our financial condition, results of operations, or financial statement disclosures.

Materiality

Material in accountant-speak means something significant—something that would affect the judgment of an informed investor about the company's financial situation. Every material event or piece of information must be disclosed, typically in the footnotes of financial statements. For example, Apple's financials for fiscal year 2011 include the following caveat:

> *As of September 24, 2011, the end of the annual period covered by this report, the Company was subject to the various legal proceedings and claims discussed below, as well as certain other legal proceedings and claims that have not been fully resolved and that have arisen in the ordinary course of business. In the opinion of management, there was not at least a reasonable possibility the Company may have incurred a material loss, or a material loss in excess of a recorded accrual, with respect to loss contingencies. However, the outcome of legal proceedings and claims brought against the Company are subject to significant uncertainty. Therefore, although management considers the likelihood of such an outcome to be remote, if one or more of these legal matters were resolved against the Company in the same reporting period for amounts in excess of management's expectations, the Company's consolidated financial statements of a particular reporting period could be materially adversely affected.*

In other words, we don't expect any losses from lawsuits, but we might be wrong.

These five principles aren't the only ones in GAAP, but in our view they are among the most important.

INTERNATIONAL STANDARDS

The rest of the world—more than one hundred countries—uses standards that are different from GAAP. They are called International Financial Reporting Standards, or IFRS. Like GAAP, IFRS lays down guidelines and rules that organizations follow when putting together their financial statements. The goal of IFRS is to make company comparisons from one country to another as easy as possible. The IFRS rules are generally somewhat simpler than GAAP's.

And as this book goes to press—guess what?—the United States may join IFRS. The AICPA has recommended that it do so, and the SEC is promising a decision soon. However, it is likely to be several years before US companies are required to abide by IFRS rules. Meanwhile, companies themselves disagree about the proposed changeover. For instance, in July 2011, a *Wall Street Journal* article reported a clash between big and small companies. Larger companies, which often do business internationally, generally want the IFRS implementation; smaller companies, often with no business outside of the United States, don't see any value.[1] From our perspective, moving to IFRS would mean that every financial statement used the same language, something we always think is a good thing.

NON-GAAP REPORTING

Remember we said at the beginning of this chapter that some companies prepare not only their regular GAAP financials but another set of statements that do not follow GAAP rules? Well, it's true. Many companies report numbers that do not fall under the rules and guidelines of GAAP. These are called—hold your breath—non-GAAP numbers. Companies often use them for internal management purposes.

Does this mean that the companies are keeping the proverbial two sets of books? Not really. They use non-GAAP numbers to understand their business, without worrying about matters such as onetime events or changes in GAAP guidelines that are irrelevant to running the company. Many companies even report non-GAAP numbers (along with their GAAP numbers) to Wall Street analysts and the public. They may believe that the non-GAAP numbers more accurately portray the company's performance, or that certain non-GAAP numbers are important measures of performance. Or they may just want to present the company's financial situation without certain numbers that are irrelevant to the long-term prospects of the business. In general, they present the non-GAAP results because they believe those numbers enhance outsiders' understanding of the company's performance and facilitate year-to-year comparisons.

Here, for example, is what Starbucks had to say in its press release announcing its results for the third quarter of 2011:

- Consolidated operating margin was 13.7%, up 120 basis points over prior-year period's GAAP results and 40 basis points over prior-year period's non-GAAP results.
- US operating margin improved 300 basis points to 18.8% on a GAAP basis and 210 basis points over the prior-year period's non-GAAP results.
- International operating margin improved 200 basis points to 12.2% on a GAAP basis and 140 basis points over the prior-year period's non-GAAP results.

A "basis point," incidentally, is one one-hundredth of a percentage point. So 100 basis points equals 1 percent. As for operating margin, you'll learn about it later in chapter 21; for now, understand that it is a measure of profit. So Starbucks is reporting profit in both GAAP and non-GAAP terms.

Later in the press release, Starbucks explains how it calculated its non-GAAP numbers:

> *The non-GAAP financial measures provided in this release exclude 2010 restructuring charges, primarily related to previously announced company-operated store closures. The company's management believes that providing these non-GAAP financial measures better enables investors to understand and evaluate the company's historical and prospective operating performance. More specifically, for historical non-GAAP financial measures, management excludes restructuring charges because it believes that these costs do not reflect expected future operating expenses and do not contribute to a meaningful evaluation of the company's future operating performance or comparisons to the company's past operating performance.*

Ironically, GAAP rules have a requirement that governs the reporting of non-GAAP numbers. Companies usually show how they got, mathematically, from the GAAP number to the non-GAAP number. This is often called a bridge statement. We aren't going to get into that here—too many details!—but feel free to look into companies' financial statement notes or supplemental documents if you're interested.

OK, enough on GAAP. Now let's plunge into the nitty-gritty of financial intelligence, beginning with the three financial statements.

Part One
Toolbox

GETTING WHAT YOU WANT

Imagine the shock on your boss's face if you made a case for a raise—and part of your case included a detailed analysis of the company's financial picture, showing exactly how your unit has contributed.

Far-fetched? Not really. Once you read this book, you'll know how to gather and interpret data such as the following:

- *The company's revenue growth, profit growth, and margin improvements over the past year.* If the business is doing well, senior managers may be thinking about new plans and opportunities. They'll need experienced people—like you.

- *The company's remaining financial challenges.* Could inventory turns be improved? What about gross margins or receivable days? If you can suggest specific ways to better the business's financial performance, both you and your boss will look smart.

- *Your company's cash flow position.* Maybe you'll be able to show that your company has lots of free cash flow for raises for its hardworking employees.

The same goes for when you apply for that next job. The experts always tell job seekers to ask questions of the interviewer—and if you ask financial questions, you'll show that you understand the financial side of the business. Try questions like these:

- Is the company profitable?
- Does it have positive equity?
- Does it have a current ratio that can support payroll?
- Are revenues growing or declining?

If you don't know how to assess all these, read the rest of this book—you'll learn.

THE PLAYERS AND WHAT THEY DO

Who's really in charge of finance and accounting? Titles and responsibilities differ from one company to another, but here's an overview of who usually does what in the upper echelons of these departments:

- *Chief financial officer (CFO).* The CFO is involved in the management and strategy of the organization from a financial perspective. He or she oversees all financial functions; the company controller and treasurer report to the CFO. The CFO is usually part of the executive committee and often sits on the board of directors. For financial matters, the buck stops here.
- *Treasurer.* The treasurer focuses outside the company as well as inside. He or she is responsible for building and maintaining banking relationships, managing cash flow, forecasting, and making equity and capital-structure decisions. The treasurer is also responsible for investor relations and stock-based equity decisions. Some would say that the ideal treasurer is a finance professional with a personality.
- *Controller.* The focus of the controller—sometimes spelled *comptroller*—is purely internal. His or her job is providing reliable and accurate financial reports. The controller is responsible for general accounting, financial reporting, business analysis, financial planning, asset management, and internal controls. He or she ensures that day-to-day transactions are recorded accurately and correctly. Without good, consistent data from the controller, the CFO and the treasurer can't

do their jobs. The controller is sometimes called a bean counter. It's wise to use this term correctly; some CFOs and treasurers get annoyed when it is used to describe them, as they do not consider themselves bean counters but financial professionals.

REPORTING OBLIGATIONS OF PUBLIC COMPANIES

Publicly traded companies—companies whose stocks anyone can buy on an exchange—must ordinarily file a number of reports with a government agency. In the United States, that agency is the Securities and Exchange Commission (SEC). Of the forms required by the SEC, the most commonly known and utilized is the annual report, known as Form 10-K or just a 10-K. This is not the same thing as the glossy brochure many companies distribute to their shareholders, which is also called an annual report. The glossy version usually features a letter from the CEO and chairman; it may also include promotional information about the company's products and services, pie charts and colored graphs, and other marketing-related content. The SEC version—the 10-K—is usually drab black and white, with pages upon pages of text and data, all required by SEC regulations. It includes items such as company history, executive compensation, risks in the business, legal proceedings, management discussion of the business, financial statements (prepared according to GAAP, as described in chapter 4), notes to the financial statements, and financial controls and procedures. You can learn a lot from it.

Public companies also must file a report known as a 10-Q every three months. The 10-Q is much shorter than the 10-K; most of it is devoted to reporting a company's financial results for the most recent quarter. Companies produce only three 10-Qs because they include the final quarter in their 10-Ks.

Note that quarter ends and year ends do not have to correspond to the calendar. The end of a company's fiscal year can be any date that the company establishes, and the quarters are calculated from that. For example, if a company's year end is January 31, then its quarters are February through April, May through July, August through October, and November through January.

You can find 10-Ks, 10-Qs, and other forms that are required SEC filings on the websites of individual companies and on the SEC's website. The latter uses a database called EDGAR and contains a tutorial on how to use it.

Part Two

The (Many) Peculiarities of the Income Statement

5

Profit Is an Estimate

IN A FAMILIAR PHRASE GENERALLY ATTRIBUTED to Peter Drucker, profit is the sovereign criterion of the enterprise. The use of the word *sovereign* is right on the money. A profitable company charts its own course. Its managers can run it the way they wish to. When a company stops being profitable, other people begin to poke their noses into the business. Profitability is also how you as a manager are likely to be judged. Are you contributing to the company's profitability or detracting from it? Are you figuring out ways to increase profitability every day, or are you just doing your job and hoping everything will work out?

Another familiar saying, this one variously attributed to Laurence J. Peter of *The Peter Principle* and to Yogi Berra, tells us that if we don't know where we're going we'll probably wind up somewhere else. If you don't know *how* to contribute to profitability, you're unlikely to do so effectively.

In fact, too many people in business don't understand what profit really *is*, let alone how it is calculated. Nor do they understand that a company's profit in any given period reflects a whole host of estimates and assumptions. The art of finance might just as easily be termed the art of making a profit—or, in some cases, the art of making profits look better than they really are. We'll see in this part of the book how companies can do this, both legally and illegally. Most companies play it pretty straight, though there are always a few that end up pushing the limits.

We'll focus on the basics of understanding an income statement, because "profit" is no more and no less than what shows up there. Learn to decipher this document, and you will be able to understand and evaluate your company's profitability. Learn to manage the lines on the income statement that you can affect, and you will know how to contribute to that profitability. Learn the art involved in determining profit, and you will definitely increase your financial intelligence. You might even get where you are going.

A (VERY) LITTLE ACCOUNTING

We promised in the previous chapter to include only a smattering of accounting procedures in this book. There is one accounting idea, however, that we will explain in this chapter, because once you understand it, you will grasp exactly what the income statement is and what it is trying to tell you. First, though, we want to back up one step and make sure there isn't a major misconception lurking in your mind.

You know that the income statement is supposed to show a company's profit for a given period—usually a month, a quarter, or a year. It's only a short leap of imagination to conclude that the income statement shows how much cash the company took in during that period, how much it spent, and how much was left over. That "left over" amount would then be the company's profit, right?

Alas, no. Except for some very small businesses that do their accounting this way—it's called *cash-based accounting*—that notion of an income statement and profit is based on a fundamental misconception. In fact, an income statement measures something quite different from cash in the door, cash out the door, and cash left over. It measures *sales* or *revenues, costs* or *expenses*, and *profit* or *income.*

Any income statement begins with sales. When a business delivers a product or a service to a customer, accountants say it has made a sale. Never mind if the customer hasn't paid for the product or service yet—the business may count the amount of the sale on the top line of its income statement for the period in question. No money at all may have changed hands. Of course, for cash-based businesses such as retailers and restaurants, sales and cash coming in are pretty much the same. But most businesses have to

The Matching Principle

The matching principle is a fundamental accounting rule for preparing an income statement. It simply states, "Match the cost with its associated revenue to determine profits in a given period of time—usually a month, quarter, or year." In other words, one of the accountants' primary jobs is to figure out and properly record all the costs incurred in generating sales.

wait thirty days or more to collect on their sales, and manufacturers of big products such as airplanes may have to wait many months. (You can see that managing a company such as Boeing would entail having a lot of cash on hand to cover payroll and operating costs until the company is paid for its work. We'll get to a concept known as working capital, which helps you assess such matters, in part 7 of the book.)

And the "cost" lines of the income statement? Well, the costs and expenses a company reports are not necessarily the ones it wrote checks for during that period. The *costs and expenses on the income statement are those it incurred in generating the sales recorded during that time period*. Accountants call this the *matching principle*—all costs should be *matched* to the associated revenue for the period represented in the income statement—and it's the key to understanding how profit is determined.

The matching principle is the little bit of accounting you need to learn. For example:

- If an ink-and-toner supplier buys a truckload of cartridges in June to resell to customers over the next several months, it does *not* record the cost of all those cartridges in June. Rather, it records the cost of each cartridge when the cartridge is sold. The reason is the matching principle.

- And if a delivery company buys a truck in January that it plans to use over the next three years, the cost of the truck doesn't show up on the income statement for January. Rather, the truck is depreciated over the whole three years, with one-thirty-sixth of the truck's cost appearing as an expense on the income statement each month (assuming simple straight-line methods of depreciation). Why? The matching principle. The truck is one of the many costs associated with the work performed during each of the thirty-six months—the work that shows up in that month's income statement.

- The matching principle even extends to items like taxes. A company may pay its tax bill once a quarter—but every month the accountants will tuck into the income statement a figure reflecting the taxes owed on that month's profits.

- The matching principle applies to service companies as well as product companies. A consulting firm, for example, sells billable hours, meaning the time each consultant is working with a client. Accountants still need to match all the expenses associated with the time—marketing costs, materials costs, research costs, and so on—to the associated revenue.

You can see how far we are from cash in and cash out. Tracking the flow of cash in and out the door is the job of another financial document, namely the cash flow statement (part 4). You can also see how far we are from simple objective reality. Accountants can't just tote up the flow of dollars; they have to *decide* which costs are associated with the sales. They have to make assumptions and come up with estimates. In the process, they may introduce bias into the numbers.

THE PURPOSE OF THE INCOME STATEMENT

In principle, the income statement tries to measure whether the products or services that a company provides are profitable when everything is added up. It's the accountants' best effort to show the sales the company generated during a given time period, the costs incurred in making those sales (including the costs of operating the business for that span of time), and the profit, if any, that is left over. Possible bias aside, this is a critically important endeavor for nearly every manager in a business. A sales manager needs to know what kind of profits she and her team are generating so that she can make decisions about discounts, terms, which customers to pursue, and so on. A marketing manager needs to know which products are most profitable so that those can be emphasized in any marketing campaigns. A human resources manager should know the profitability of products so that he knows where the company's strategic priorities are likely to lie when he is recruiting new people.

Over time, the income statement and the cash flow statement in a well-run company will track one another. *Profit* will be turned into *cash*. As we saw in chapter 3, however, just because a company is making a profit in any given time period doesn't mean it will have the cash to pay its bills. Profit is always an estimate—and you can't spend estimates.

With that lesson under our belts, let's turn to the business of decoding the income statement.

6

Cracking the Code of the Income Statement

NOTE THAT WORD WE USED IN THE TITLE to this chapter: *code.* Unfortunately, an income statement can often seem like a code that needs to be deciphered.

Here's the reason. In books like this one—and even later in this book—you will often find cute little sample income statements. They look something like this:

Revenues	$100
Cost of goods sold	50
Gross profit	50
Expenses	30
Taxes	5
Net profit	$ 15

A bright fourth-grader wouldn't need much help figuring out that one, once she had a little help with definitions. She could even do the math without a calculator. But now check out a real-world income statement—your own company's or one that you find in some other company's annual report. If it's a detailed statement used internally, it may go on literally for pages—line after line after line of numbers, usually in print so small you can barely read them. Even if it's a "consolidated" statement like those you find in annual reports, it's likely to contain a whole bunch of lines with arcane labels like "income from equity affiliates" (that's from Exxon Mobil) or "amortization of purchased intangible assets" (from Hewlett-Packard). It's enough to make anybody but a financial professional throw up his hands in dismay (and many of the pros get confused, too).

So bear with us while we run through some simple procedures for curling up with an income statement. Boosting your financial intelligence shouldn't involve an attack of heartburn, and learning these steps may save you from just that.

READING AN INCOME STATEMENT

Before you even start contemplating the numbers, you need some context for understanding the document.

The Label

Does it say "income statement" at the top? It may not. It may instead say "profit and loss statement" or "P&L statement," "operating statement" or "statement of operations," "statement of earnings" or "earnings statement." All these terms refer to the same document. Often the word *consolidated* appears as part of the title. If it does, you are probably looking at an income statement for a whole company, with totals for major categories rather than highly detailed line items.

The many different names for an income statement could drive a person nuts. We work with a client that calls the income statement in its annual report the statement of earnings. Meanwhile, one of the company's major divisions calls its income statement an income statement—and another major division calls it the profit and loss statement! With all these terms for the same thing, one might get the idea that our friends in finance and accounting don't want us to know what is going on. Or maybe they just take it for granted that everybody knows that all the different terms mean the same thing. However that may be, in this book we will always use the term *income statement*.

Incidentally, if you see "balance sheet" or "statement of cash flows" at the top, you have the wrong document. The label pretty much has to include one of those phrases we just mentioned.

What It's Measuring

Is this income statement for an entire company? Is it for a division or business unit? Is it for a region? Larger companies typically produce income statements not just for the whole organization but also for various parts of the business, right down to individual stores, plants, or product lines. H. Thomas Johnson and Robert S. Kaplan, in their classic book *Relevance Lost*, tell how General Motors developed the divisional system—with income statements for each division—in the first half of the twentieth century.[1] We can be glad it did. Creating income statements for smaller business units has provided managers in large corporations with enormous insights into their units' financial performance. Remember that these division or business-unit financial statements usually require allocations or estimates for costs that apply to more than one division or unit.

Once you have identified the relevant entity, you need to check the time period. An income statement, like a report card in school, is always for a span of time: a month, quarter, or year, or maybe year-to-date. Some companies produce income statements for a time span as short as a week. Incidentally, the figures on large companies' income statements are usually rounded off and the last zeros are left off. So look for a little note at the top: "in millions" (add six zeros to the numbers) or "in thousands" (add three zeros). This may sound like common sense, and indeed it is. But we have found that seemingly trivial details such as this are often overlooked by financial newcomers.

"Actual" Versus "Pro Forma"

Most income statements are *actual*, and if there's no other label, you can assume that is what you're looking at. They show what "actually" happened to revenues, costs, and profits during that time period. If you are looking at a public company's statement, you can assume it has been compiled according to the generally accepted principles of accounting (GAAP). If it is a privately held company, one of the questions you'll need to ask is whether the numbers are based on GAAP principles. (We put "actually" in quotes to remind you that *any* income statement has those built-in estimates, assumptions, and biases, which we will discuss in more detail later in this part of the book.)

There are also pro forma and non-GAAP income statements. *Pro forma* means that the income statement is a projection. If you are drawing up a plan for a new business, for instance, you might write down a projected income statement for the first year or two—in other words, what you hope and expect will happen in terms of sales and costs. That projection is called a pro forma. A *non-GAAP* income statement may exclude any unusual or one-time charges, or it may relax some GAAP rules. (See chapter 4 for more detail.) Say a company has to take a big write-off in a particular year, resulting in a loss on the bottom line. (More on write-offs later in this part.) Along with its actual income statement, it might prepare one that shows what would have happened without the write-off. To add to the confusion, many companies used to call these non-GAAP statements pro forma income statements. Today that term is reserved for projections.

Pro forma income statements—projections—are of course just that. They are educated guesses about the future. Non-GAAP income statements are different. They reflect reality, but they have to be interpreted with care. When companies prepare such documents for public consumption, the ostensible purpose is to let you compare last year (when there was no write-off) with this year (if there hadn't been that ugly write-off). But sometimes there is a subliminal message, something along the lines of, "Hey, things aren't really as bad as they look—we just lost money because of that write-off." Of course, the write-off really did happen, and the company really did lose money. Most of the time, you want to look at the GAAP as well as the non-GAAP statements, and if you have to choose just one, the GAAP statement is probably the better bet. Cynics sometimes describe non-GAAP statements as income statements with all the bad stuff taken out. That's not always fair—but sometimes it is.

The Big Numbers

No matter whose income statement you're looking at, there will be three main categories. One is *sales*, which may be called *revenue* (it's the same thing). Sales or revenue is always at the top. When people refer to "top-line growth," that's what they mean: sales growth. Costs and expenses are in the middle, and profit is at the bottom. (If the income statement you're looking at is for a nonprofit, "profit" may be called "surplus/deficit" or "net revenue.") There are subsets of profit that may be listed as you go along, too—gross profit, for example. We'll explain all of these in chapter 9.

You can usually tell what's important to a company by looking at the biggest numbers relative to sales. For example, the sales line is usually followed by "cost of goods sold," or COGS. In a service business, the line is often "cost of services," or COS. Occasionally, you might also see "cost of revenue." If that line is a large fraction of sales, you can bet that management in that company watches COGS or COS *very* closely. In your own company, you will want to know exactly what is included in line items that are relevant to your job. If you're a sales manager, for instance, you'll need to find out exactly what goes into the line labeled "selling expense." As we'll see, accountants have some discretion as to how they categorize various expenses.

By the way: unless you're a financial professional, you can usually ignore items like "amortization of purchased intangible assets." Most lines with labels like that aren't material to the bottom line anyway. And if they are, they ought to be explained in the footnotes.

Comparative Data

The consolidated income statements presented in annual reports typically have three columns of figures, reflecting what happened during the past three years. Internal income statements may have many more columns. You may see something like this, for example:

Actual % of sales	Budget % of sales	Variance %

Or like this:

Actual previous period	$ Change (+/–)	% Change

Tables of numbers like these can be intimidating. But they don't need to be.

In the first case, "% of sales" is simply a way of showing the magnitude of an expense number relative to revenue. The revenue line is taken as a given—a fixed point—and everything else is compared with it. Many companies set percent-of-sales targets for given line items, and then take action if they miss the target by a significant amount. For instance, maybe senior executives have decided that selling expenses shouldn't be more than 12 percent of sales. If the number creeps up much above 12 percent, the sales organization had better watch out. It's the same with the budget and variance numbers. ("Variance" just means difference.) If the actual number is way off budget—that is, if the variance is high—you can be sure that somebody will want to know why. Financially savvy managers always identify variances to budget and find out why they occurred.

In the second case, the statement simply shows how the company is doing compared with last quarter or last year. Sometimes the point of comparison will be "same quarter last year." Again, if a number has moved in the wrong direction by a sizable amount, someone will want to know why.

In short, the point of these comparative income statements is to highlight what is changing, which numbers are where they are supposed to be, and which ones are not.

Footnotes

An internal income statement may or may not include footnotes. If it does, we recommend reading them very carefully. They are probably going to tell you something that the accountants think everybody should be aware of. External income statements, like those found in annual reports, are a little different. They usually include many, many footnotes. You may want to scan them: some may be interesting, others not so much.

Why all the footnotes? In cases where there is any question, the rules of accounting require the financial folks to explain how they arrived at their totals. So most of the notes are like windows into how the numbers were determined. Some are simple and straightforward, such as the following from Walmart's Form 10-K (the annual report required by the Securities and Exchange Commission) for the year ended January 31, 2011:

> *Cost of Sales*
>
> *Cost of sales includes actual product cost, the cost of transportation to the Company's warehouses, stores and clubs from suppliers, the cost of transportation from the Company's warehouses to the stores and clubs and the*

cost of warehousing for our Sam's Club segment and import distribution centers.

But other footnotes can be long and complex, such as the following footnote fragment from Hewlett-Packard's Form 10-K for the fiscal year ending October 31, 2010:

HP's current revenue recognition policies, which were applied in fiscal 2010 and fiscal 2009, provide that, when a sales arrangement contains multiple elements, such as hardware and software products, licenses and/or services, HP allocates revenue to each element based on a selling price hierarchy. The selling price for a deliverable is based on its vendor specific objective evidence ("VSOE") if available, third party evidence ("TPE") if VSOE is not available, or estimated selling price ("ESP") if neither VSOE nor TPE is available. In multiple element arrangements where more-than-incidental software deliverables are included, revenue is allocated to each separate unit of accounting for each of the non-software deliverables and to the software deliverables as a group using the relative selling prices of each of the deliverables in the arrangement based on the aforementioned selling price hierarchy. If the arrangement contains more than one software deliverable, the arrangement consideration allocated to the software deliverables as a group is then allocated to each software deliverable using the guidance for recognizing software revenue, as amended.

This is one of nine paragraphs describing revenue recognition, a topic we discuss in chapter 7. Don't get us wrong: it's important that Hewlett-Packard explain its approach to the issue. Decisions about when revenue is recognized are a key element of the art of finance. Nor should you assume that Walmart always has simple footnotes and Hewlett-Packard always has complex ones. Our examples here merely illustrate the diversity of the types of footnotes you'll find relating to the income statement in an annual report. Sometimes you find out some very interesting things about companies by reading the footnotes, so have fun! (Did we just say that footnotes can be fun?) Incidentally, if you can't find the explanations you need in the notes, ask your CFO. He ought to have the answers.

ONE BIG RULE

So those are the rules for reading. But don't forget the *one big rule* that should be in the forefront of your thinking whenever you confront an income statement. That rule says:

> *Remember that many numbers on the income statement reflect estimates and assumptions. Accountants have decided to include some transactions here and not there. They have decided to estimate one way and not another.*

That is the art of finance. If you remember this one point, we assure you that your financial intelligence already exceeds that of many managers.

So let's take a more detailed look at some of the key categories. If you don't have another income statement handy, use the sample in the appendix for reference. Sure, it will all seem complicated at first. But you will soon grow accustomed to the format and the terminology. As you do, you'll find that you are beginning to understand what the income statement is telling you.

7

Revenue

The Issue Is Recognition

WE'LL BEGIN AT THE TOP. We already noted that *sales*—the top line of an income statement—is also often called *revenue*. So far so good: only two words for the same thing isn't too bad, and we'll use both, just because they're so common. But watch out: some companies (and many people) call that top line "income." In fact, the popular accounting software QuickBooks labels it income. Most banks and financial institutions also call it income. That's *really* confusing because "income" more often means "profit," which is the *bottom* line. (Obviously, we have an uphill battle here. Where are the language police when you need them?)

A company can *record* or *recognize* a sale when it delivers a product or service to a customer. That's a simple principle. But as we suggested earlier in the book, when you put it into practice, you immediately run into complexity. In fact, the issue of when a sale can be recorded is one of the more artful aspects of the income statement. It's the one where accountants have the most discretion and that managers therefore must understand most closely. So this is one place where your skills as an educated consumer of the financials will come in handy. If things don't seem right, ask questions—and if you can't get satisfactory answers, it might be time to be concerned. Revenue recognition is a common arena for financial fraud.

Sales

Sales or revenue is the dollar value of all the products or services a company provided to its customers during a given period of time.

MURKY GUIDELINES

The most important GAAP guideline that accountants rely on for recording or recognizing a sale is that the revenue must have been *earned.* A products company must have shipped the product. A service company must have performed the work. Fair enough—but what would you do about these situations?

- Your company does systems integration for large customers. A typical project requires six months to design and be approved by the customer, then another twelve months to implement. The customer gets no real value from the project until the whole thing is complete. When have you earned the revenue that the project generates?
- Your company sells to retailers. Using a practice known as bill-and-hold, you allow your customers to buy product (say, a popular Christmas item) well in advance of the time they will actually need it. You warehouse it for them and ship it out later. When have you earned the revenue?
- You work for an architectural firm. The firm provides clients with plans for buildings, deals with the local building authorities, and supervises the construction or reconstruction. All these services are included in the firm's fee, which is generally figured as a percentage of construction costs. How do you determine when the firm has earned its revenue?

We can't provide exact answers to these questions, because accounting practices differ from one company to another. But that's precisely the point: there are no hard-and-fast answers. Project-based companies typically have rules allowing partial revenue recognition when a project reaches certain milestones. But the rules can vary. The "sales" figure on a company's top line always reflects the accountants' judgments about when they should recognize revenue. And where there is judgment, there is room for dispute—not to say manipulation.

POSSIBILITIES FOR MANIPULATION

In fact, the pressures for manipulation can be intense. Let's take a software company, for example. And let's say that it sells software along with maintenance-and-upgrade contracts extending over a period of five years. So it has to make a judgment about when to recognize revenue from a sale.

Now suppose this software company is actually a division of a large corporation, one that makes earnings predictions to Wall Street. The folks in the corporate office want to keep Wall Street happy. This quarter, alas, it looks as if the parent company is going to miss its earnings per share forecast by just a little bit. If it does, Wall Street will not be happy. And when Wall Street isn't happy, the company's stock gets hammered.

Aha! (You can hear the folks in the corporate office thinking.) Here is this software division. Suppose we change how its revenue is recognized? Suppose we recognize 75 percent up front instead of 50 percent? The logic might be that a sale in this business takes a lot of initial work, so they should recognize the cost and effort of making the sale as well as the cost of providing the product and delivering the service. Make the change—recognize the extra revenue—and suddenly earnings per share are nudged up to where Wall Street expects them to be.

Earnings per Share

Earnings per share (EPS) is a company's net profit divided by the number of shares outstanding. It's one of the numbers that Wall Street watches most closely. Wall Street has "expectations" for many companies' EPS, and if the expectations aren't met, the share price is likely to drop.

Interestingly, such a change is not illegal. An explanation might appear in a footnote to the financial statements, but then again it might not. Maybe you noticed in chapter 6 that the Hewlett-Packard footnote regarding revenue recognition policy mentioned 2009 and 2010. That's because later in that same section the company describes what it did differently in 2008:

> *For fiscal 2008 . . . HP allocated revenue to each element based on its relative fair value, or for software, based on VSOE of fair value. In the absence of fair value for a delivered element, HP first allocated revenue to the fair value of the undelivered elements and the residual revenue to the delivered elements . . .*

. . . And so on, for many more lines.

As we mentioned in chapter 4, any accounting change that is "material" to the bottom line must be footnoted in this manner. But who decides what is material and what isn't? You guessed it: the accountants. In fact, it could very well be that recognizing 75 percent up front presents a more accurate picture of the software division's reality. But was the change in accounting method due to good financial analysis, or did it reflect the need to make the earnings forecast? Could there be a bias lurking in here? Remember, accounting is the art of using limited data to come as close as possible to an accurate description of how well a company is performing. Revenue on the income statement is an estimate, a best guess. This example shows how estimates can introduce bias.

It isn't just investors who have to be careful about bias; managers, too, need to be aware of it because it can directly affect their jobs. Say you're a sales manager, and you and your staff focus on the revenue numbers every month. You manage your people based on those numbers. You talk with them about their performance. You make decisions about hiring and firing, and you hand out rewards and recognition, all according to the numbers. Now your company does what the software company did: it changes the way it recognizes revenue in order to achieve some corporate goal. Suddenly it looks as if your staff is doing great! Bonuses for everyone! But be careful: the underlying revenue figures might not look so good if they were recognized in the same way as before. If you didn't know the policy had changed and you began passing out bonuses, you'd be paying for no real improvement. Financial intelligence in this case means understanding how the revenue is recognized, analyzing the real variances in the sales figures, and paying bonuses (or not) based on true changes in performance.

Just as an aside, the most common source of accounting fraud has been and probably always will be in that top line: sales. Many companies play with revenue recognition in questionable ways. The issue is particularly acute in the software industry. Software companies often sell their products to resellers, who then sell the products to end users. Manufacturers, under pressure from Wall Street to make their numbers, are frequently tempted to ship unordered software to these distributors at the end of a quarter. (The practice is known as *channel stuffing.*) And it isn't just software. Vitesse Semiconductor, for instance, was charged by the Securities and Exchange Commission in 2010 for a series of practices conducted by its then–executive team from 1995 to 2006. Among the charges: "an elaborate channel stuffing scheme in order to improperly record revenue on product shipments." The distributor to which Vitesse shipped its wares had an "unconditional right" to send the goods back, a right established through "side letters and oral agreements." Vitesse and the executives settled the charges, and the company later acknowledged that it had "utilized improper accounting practices primarily related to revenue recognition and inventory, and prepared or altered financial records to conceal those practices." A new management team subsequently cleaned things up.[1]

One company that always took the high road in regard to this practice was Macromedia, creators of the Internet Flash player and other products. When channel stuffing was becoming a serious problem in the industry, Macromedia voluntarily reported estimates of inventory held by its distributors, thereby showing that the channels for its products were not artificially loaded up. The message was clear to shareholders and employees alike: Macromedia was not going to be dragged into this practice. (Macromedia has since been acquired by Adobe.)

The next time you read about a financial scandal, check first to see whether somebody was messing around with the revenue numbers. Unfortunately, it is all too common.

BACKLOG AND BOOKINGS

Fraud and manipulation aside, revenue shows the dollar volume of the goods or services the company has delivered to its customers. But it's not the only significant measure of a company's sales success. Equally important, in many cases, are the orders that have been signed but not yet started, or the revenue not yet recognized on partially completed projects. This is the value, in other words, of what's in the pipeline. Companies variously refer to these not-yet-recognized sales as *backlog* or *bookings.*

Many public companies report backlog or bookings to help keep analysts and shareholders informed about the companies' future prospects. They may publish the figures in a variety of ways. One of our clients, for example, tracks both the total value of its contracts and the annual value. Of course, bookings can change from one day to the next as new orders come in, existing orders are canceled or amended, and work proceeds on partially completed projects.

In some cases, you may have to ask questions to determine what a particular trend in backlog or bookings means. For example, a growing backlog might indicate increasing sales—or it might mean that the company is experiencing production problems. A falling backlog might indicate declining sales or greater production capacity. One metric that can help you figure out what's going on is the company's assessment of how much of the backlog will convert to sales in a given period of time. A company might say, for instance, that it expects approximately 75 percent of the backlog to turn into sales in the following six months.

DEFERRED REVENUE

When you buy an airplane ticket, the airline charges your credit card immediately, even if you are not planning to fly for another three weeks. Accountants call such funds *deferred revenue.*

Because of its name, deferred revenue sounds like something we should discuss in this chapter. Deferred revenue is indeed related to revenue—it will turn into revenue eventually—but it does not belong here. Remember the GAAP principle of conservatism? It says, in part, that revenue should be recognized when (and only when) it is actually earned. Deferred revenue is money that has come in but is as yet unearned. So it can't go into the income statement. Instead, accountants put deferred revenue on the balance sheet as a liability—that is, an amount that the company owes to somebody else. In the example, the airline owes you a flight. We'll discuss deferred revenue further in part 3.

8

Costs and Expenses

No Hard-and-Fast Rules

MOST MANAGERS HAVE plenty of personal experience with expenses. But did you know that there are plenty of estimates and potential biases on those expense lines? Let's examine the major line items.

COST OF GOODS SOLD OR COST OF SERVICES

As you probably do know, expenses on the income statement fall into two basic categories. The first is *cost of goods sold*, or COGS. As usual, there are a couple of different names for this category—in a service company, for instance, it may be called cost of services (COS). We've also frequently seen cost of revenue and cost of sales. For simplicity's sake, we'll use the acronyms COGS or COS. At any rate, what matters isn't the label, it's what's

Cost of Goods Sold (COGS) and Cost of Services (COS)

Cost of goods sold or cost of services is one category of expenses. It includes all the costs directly involved in producing a product or delivering a service.

included. The idea behind COGS is to measure all the costs directly associated with making the product or delivering the service. The materials. The labor. If you suspect that rule is open to a ton of interpretation, you're on the money. The accounting department has to make decisions about what to include in COGS and what to put somewhere else.

Some of these decisions are easy. In a manufacturing company, for instance, the following costs are definitely in:

- The wages of the people on the manufacturing line
- The cost of the materials that are used to make the product

And plenty of costs are definitely out, such as:

- The cost of supplies used by the accounting department (paper, etc.)
- The salary of the human resources manager in the corporate office

Ah, but then there's the gray area—and it's enormous. For example:

- What about the salary of the person who manages the plant that manufactures the product?
- What about the wages of the plant supervisors?
- What about sales commissions?

Are all of these directly related to the manufacturing of the product? Or are they indirect expenses, like the cost of the HR manager? There's the same ambiguity in a service environment. COS in a service company typically includes the labor associated with delivering the service. But what about the group supervisor? You could argue that his salary is part of general operations and therefore shouldn't be included in the COS line. You could also argue that he is supporting direct-service employees, so he should be included with them in that line. These are all judgment calls. There are no hard-and-fast rules.

The fact that there aren't any, frankly, is a little surprising. GAAP runs for many thousands of pages and spells out a *lot* of detailed rules. You'd think GAAP would say, "The plant manager is out," or "The supervisor is in." No such luck; GAAP only provides guidelines. Companies take those guidelines and apply a logic that makes sense for their particular situations. The key, as accountants like to say, is reasonableness and consistency. So long as a company's logic is reasonable, and so long as that logic is applied consistently, whatever it wants to do is OK.

As to why a manager should care what's in and what's out, consider the following scenarios:

- You run the engineering analysis department at an architectural firm, and in the past your staff's salaries have been included in COS. Now the finance folks are moving all those costs out of COS. It's perfectly reasonable—even though your department has a lot to do with completing an architectural design, a case can be made that it isn't *directly* related to any particular job. So does the change matter? You bet. You and your staff are no longer part of what's often called "above the line." That means you're going to show up differently on the corporate radar screen. If your company focuses on gross profit, for instance, management will be monitoring COS carefully. It will try to ensure that departments affecting COS have everything they need to hit their targets. Once you're outside of COS—"below the line"—the level of attention may be significantly lower.
- You're a plant manager charged with making a gross profit of $1 million per month. This month you're $20,000 short. Then you realize that $25,000 of your COGS is in a line item labeled "contract administration on plant orders." Does that really belong in COGS? You

Above the Line, Below the Line

The "line" generally refers to gross profit. Above that line on the income statement, typically, are sales and COGS or COS. Below the line are operating expenses, interest, and taxes. What's the difference? Items listed above the line tend to vary more (in the short term) than many of those below the line, and so tend to get more managerial attention.

petition the controller to move those costs to operating expenses. Your controller agrees; the change is done. You hit your target, and everyone is happy. An outsider might even look at what's happening and believe that gross margins are improving—all from a change you made because you were trying to hit a target.

Again, these changes are legal, so long as they meet the reasonable-and-consistent test. You can even take an expense out of COGS one month and petition to put it back in next month. All you need is a reason good enough to convince the controller (and the auditor, if the changes are material)—and you need to disclose the change if it's material. Of course, changing the rules constantly from one period to the next would be bad form. One thing we all need from our accountants is consistency.

OPERATING EXPENSES: WHAT'S NECESSARY?

And where do costs go when they are taken out of COGS? Where is "below the line?" That's the other basic category of costs, namely operating expenses. Some companies refer to operating expenses as sales, general, and administrative expenses (SG&A, or just G&A), while others treat G&A as one subcategory and give sales and marketing its own line. Often a company will base this distinction on the relative size of each. Microsoft chooses to show sales and marketing on a separate line because sales and marketing are a significant portion of the company's expenses. By contrast, the biotech firm Genentech includes sales and marketing with G&A, the more typical approach. Both companies separate out R&D costs because of their relative importance. So pay attention to how your company organizes these expenses.

Operating Expenses (Once More)

Operating expenses are the other major category of expenses. The category includes costs that are not directly related to making the product or delivering a service.

Operating expenses are often thought of and referred to as "overhead." The category includes items such as rent, utilities, telephone, research, and marketing. It also includes management and staff salaries—HR, accounting, IT, and so forth—plus everything else that the accountants have decided does not belong in COGS.

You can think of operating expenses as the cholesterol in a business. Good cholesterol makes you healthy, while bad cholesterol clogs your arteries. Good operating expenses make your business strong, and bad operating expenses drag down your bottom line and prevent you from taking advantage of business opportunities. (Another name for bad operating expenses is "unnecessary bureaucracy." Also "lard." You can probably come up with others.)

One more thing about COGS and operating expenses. You might think that COGS is the same as "variable costs"—costs that vary with the volume of production—and that operating expenses are fixed costs. Materials, for example, are a variable cost: the more you produce, the more material you have to buy. And materials are included in COGS. The salaries of the people in the HR department are fixed costs, and they're included in operating expenses. Unfortunately, things aren't so simple here, either. For example, if the supervisors' salaries are included in COGS, then that line item is fixed in the short run, whether you turn out one hundred thousand widgets or one hundred fifty thousand. Or take selling expenses, which are typically part of SG&A. If you have a commissioned sales force, sales expenses are to some extent variable, but they are included in operating expenses, rather than COGS.

THE POWER OF DEPRECIATION AND AMORTIZATION

Another part of operating expenses that is often buried in that SG&A line is depreciation and amortization. How this expense is treated can *greatly* affect the profit on an income statement.

We described an example of depreciation earlier in this part—buying a delivery truck and then spreading the cost over the three-year period that we assume the truck will be used for. As we said, that's an example of the matching principle. In general, depreciation is the "expensing" of a physical asset, such as a truck or a machine, over its estimated useful life. All this means is that the accountants figure out how long the asset is likely to be in use, take the appropriate fraction of its total cost, and count that amount as an expense on the income statement.

In those few dry sentences, however, lurks a powerful tool that financial artists can put to work. It's worth going into some detail here, because you'll see exactly how assumptions about depreciation can affect any company's bottom line.

To keep things simple, let's assume we start a delivery company and line up a few customers. In the first full month of operation we do $10,000 worth of business. We also incur $5,000 in direct costs (drivers' wages, gas, etc.) and $3,000 in overhead costs (rent, marketing expense, and so on). At the start of that month, our company bought one of those $36,000 trucks to make the deliveries. Since we're expecting the truck to last three years, we depreciate it at $1,000 a month (using the simple straight-line depreciation approach).

So a greatly simplified income statement might look like this:

Revenues	$10,000
Cost of goods sold	5,000
Gross profit	5,000
Expenses	3,000
Depreciation	1,000
Net profit	$ 1,000

But our accountants don't have a crystal ball. They don't *know* that the truck will last exactly three years. That's an assumption they're making. Consider some alternative assumptions:

- They might assume the truck will last only one year, in which case they have to depreciate it at $3,000 a month. That takes $2,000 off the bottom line and moves the company from a net profit of $1,000 to a *loss* of $1,000.

- Alternatively, they could assume that it will last six years (seventy-two months). In that case, depreciation is only $500 a month, and net profit jumps to $1,500.

Hmm. In the former case, we're suddenly operating in the red. In the latter, we have increased net profit 50 percent. *And it's all just from changing one assumption about depreciation.* Accountants have to follow GAAP, of course, but GAAP allows plenty of flexibility. No matter what set of rules the accountants follow, estimating will be required whenever an asset lasts longer than a single accounting period. The job for the financially intelligent manager is to understand those estimates and to know how they affect the financials.

If you think this is purely an academic exercise, consider the famous example of Waste Management Inc. (WMI). WMI was once a great corporate success story, a leader in the business of hauling trash. So it came as a shock to everybody when the company announced that it would take a pretax charge—a one-time write-off—of $3.54 *billion* against its earnings. Sometimes one-time charges are taken in advance of a restructuring, as we'll discuss later in this chapter. But this was different. In effect, WMI was admitting that it had been cooking its books on a previously unimaginable scale. It had actually earned $3.54 billion less in the previous several years than it had reported during that time.

What was going on? WMI had originally grown by buying up other garbage companies. Its growth was rapid, and the company became a darling of Wall Street. When the supply of garbage companies to buy began to dwindle, it bought companies in other industries. But while it was pretty good at hauling trash, it didn't know how to run those other companies effectively. WMI's profit margins declined. Its share price plummeted. Desperate to prop up the stock, executives began looking for ways to increase earnings.

Their gaze fell first on their fleet of twenty thousand garbage trucks, for which they'd paid an average of $150,000 apiece. Up to that point, the company had been depreciating the trucks over eight to ten years, which was the standard practice in the industry. That period wasn't long enough, the executives decided. A good truck could last twelve, thirteen, even fourteen years. When you add four years to your truck depreciation schedule, you can do wonderful things to your bottom line; it's like the little example of the delivery company multiplied thousands of times over. But the executives didn't stop there. They realized that they had other assets they could do the same tricks with—about 1.5 million Dumpsters, for example. You could extend each Dumpster's depreciation period from the standard twelve years to, say, fifteen, eighteen, or twenty years, and you'd pick up another chunk of earnings per year. By fiddling with the depreciation numbers on the trucks and the Dumpsters, Waste Management's executives were able to pump up pretax earnings by a whopping $716 million. And this was just one of many tricks they used to make profits look larger than they were, which is why the end total was so huge.

Of course, the whole tangled web eventually came unraveled, as fraudulent schemes usually do. By then, however, it was too late to save the company. It was sold to a competitor, which kept the name but changed just about everything else. As for the perpetrators of the fraud, no criminal charges were ever filed against them, although some civil penalties were assessed.

Depreciation is a prime example of what accountants call a *noncash expense*. Right here, of course, is where they often lose the rest of us. How can an expense be other than cash? The key to that puzzling term is to remember that the cash has probably already been paid. The company already bought the truck. But the expense wasn't recorded that month, so it has to be allocated over the truck's life, a little at a time. No more money is going out the door; rather, it's just the accountant's way of figuring that *this* month's revenue depends on using that truck, so the income statement had better have something in it that reflects the truck's cost. Incidentally, you should know that there are many methods to determine how to depreciate an asset. You don't need to know what they are; you can leave that to the accountants. All you need to know is whether the use of the asset is matched appropriately to the revenue it is bringing in.

Amortization is the same basic idea as depreciation, but it applies to intangible assets. These days, intangible assets are often a big part of com-

Noncash Expense

A noncash expense is one that is charged to a period on the income statement but is not actually paid out in cash. An example is depreciation: accountants deduct a certain amount each month for depreciation of equipment, but the company isn't obliged to pay out that amount, because the equipment was acquired in a previous period.

panies' balance sheets. Items such as patents, copyrights, and goodwill (to be explained in chapter 11) are all assets—they cost money to acquire, and they have value—but they aren't physical assets like real estate and equipment. Still, they must be accounted for in a similar way. Take a patent. Your company had to buy the patent, or it had to do the research and development that lies behind it and then apply for it. Now the patent is helping to bring in revenue. So the company must match the expense of the patent with the revenue it helps to bring in, a little bit at a time. When an asset is intangible, though, accountants call that process amortization rather than depreciation. We're not sure why—but whatever the reason, it's a source of confusion.

Incidentally, economic depreciation implies that an asset loses its value over time. And indeed: a truck used in a delivery business does lose its value as it get older. But accounting depreciation and amortization are more about cost allocation than about loss of value. A truck, for example, may be depreciated over three years so that its accounting value at the end of that time is zero. But it may still have some value on the open market at the end of that time. A patent may be amortized over its useful life, but if technology has advanced beyond it, the patent's value may be close to zero after a couple of years, regardless of what the accountants say. So assets are rarely worth what the books say they are worth. (We'll discuss accounting or "book" value in greater detail in part 3.)

ONE-TIME CHARGES: A YELLOW FLAG

Accounting is like life in at least one respect: there's a lot of stuff that doesn't fall neatly into categories. So every income statement has a big group of expenses that do not fall into COGS and are not operating expenses either. Every statement is different, but typically you'll see lines for "other income/expense" (usually this is gain or loss from selling assets, or from transactions unrelated to the everyday operations of the business) and of course "taxes." Most of these you don't need to worry about. But there is one line that often turns up after COGS and operating expenses (though it is sometimes included under operating expenses)—a line you should definitely understand because it is often critical to profitability. The most common label for this line is "one-time charge."

You may occasionally have seen the phrase *taking the big bath* or something similar in the *Wall Street Journal.* That's a reference to these one-time charges, which are also known as *extraordinary items, write-offs, write-downs,* or *restructuring charges.* Sometimes write-offs occur, as in Waste Management's case, when a company has been doing something wrong and wants to correct its books. More often, one-time charges occur when a new CEO takes over a company and wants to restructure, reorganize, close plants, and maybe lay people off. It's the CEO's attempt, right or wrong, to improve the company based on his assessment of what the company needs. (Sometimes it's also an attempt to blame the company's performance on the previous CEO and thus to garner credit for performance improvements in a subsequent year.) Normally, such a restructuring entails a lot of costs—paying off leases, offering severance packages, disposing of facilities, selling off equipment, and so on. GAAP requires accountants to record expenses as soon as they know that expenses will be incurred, even if they have to estimate exactly what the final figure will be. So when a restructuring occurs, accountants need to estimate those charges and record them.

Here is a real yellow flag—a truly terrific place for bias in the numbers to show up. After all, how do you really estimate the cost of restructuring? Accountants have a lot of discretion, and they're liable to be off the mark in one direction or another. If their estimate is too high—that is, if the actual costs are lower than expected—then part of that one-time charge has to be "reversed." A reversed charge actually adds to profit in the new time period, so profits in that period wind up *higher* than they would otherwise have been—and all because an accounting estimate in a previous period was inaccurate! "Chainsaw Al" Dunlap, the notorious CEO of Sunbeam, was said to regard his accounting department as a profit center, and this may suggest why. (Incidentally, if you ever hear a senior executive refer to the accounting department in this manner, your company might have a problem.)

Of course, maybe the restructuring charge is too small. Then another charge has to be taken later. That clouds the numbers, because the charge isn't really matched to any revenue in the new time period. This time around, profits are lower than they otherwise would be, again because the accountants made the wrong estimate in an earlier time frame. Some years ago, AT&T seemed to be taking "one-time" restructuring charges frequently over an extended period. The company kept saying that earnings *before* the restructuring charge were growing—but it didn't make much difference, because after all those restructuring charges, the company was in pretty rough shape financially. Besides, if a company takes extraordinary one-time restructuring charges for several years in a row, how extraordinary can those charges really be? Walter Schuetze, former chief accountant for the Securities and Exchange Commission, said at the time that such charges have the effect of "deluding the investor into thinking that things are really better than they are."[1]

TRACKING EXPENSES DIFFERENTLY DEPENDING ON WHO'S LOOKING

This section isn't about fraud. It isn't even about trying to make things look better than they are within the rules. This is about who is looking at the numbers and what the numbers are used for. Most companies track expenses in at least two ways. Some track them in more than two, all for the purpose of following rules and using financial information to manage the business.

How can this be? For one thing, GAAP guidelines do have something to say about how expenses are shown on the income statement. The categories, and what goes into them, are based on guidelines that allow for consistency, conservatism, matching, and the other GAAP principles and guidelines. Companies then make determinations within the guidelines as to how to show expenses in their public statements. For example, Coca-Cola shows the following expenses in its public GAAP income statement:

- Cost of goods sold
- Selling, general, and administrative
- Other operating charges
- Interest expense
- Income taxes

All well and good, but would these categories really help a manager run her unit? We aren't privy to Coca-Cola's internal income statements, but here are a few of the categories we suspect many managers (both of the parent corporation and the bottling units) would need to understand. They would want to know, for instance, how much they were spending on:

- Each ingredient used to make the beverages, broken down by beverage
- All the costs related to delivering the product, in sufficient detail so that the costs could be managed
- Departmental costs, such as accounting, human resources, IT, and so on
- Sales and marketing costs broken down by product, advertising campaign, and more

Finally, some companies share what they reported to the government on their tax returns. These numbers are probably the farthest away from what is useful to a manager. Tax returns follow tax rules, which are not the same as GAAP rules. The returns were probably prepared by tax accountants, a subspecialty of the profession. So tax returns look different from conventional financial statements. It isn't fraud, it's just different ways of looking at the same reality.

9

The Many Forms of Profit

SO FAR WE HAVE COVERED SALES OR REVENUE—the top line—and costs and expenses. Revenue minus costs and expenses equals profit.

Of course, it might also equal *earnings, income,* or even *margin.* Amazingly enough, some companies use all these different terms for *profit,* sometimes in the same document. An income statement might have items labeled "gross margin," "operating income," "net profit," and "earnings per share." All these are the different types of profit typically seen on an income statement—and the company could just as easily have said "gross profit," "operating profit," "net profit," and "profit per share." When they use different words right there in the same statement, it looks as if they are talking about different concepts. But they aren't.

So let's always use the term *profit* here, and look at its various incarnations.

GROSS PROFIT: HOW MUCH IS ENOUGH?

Gross profit—revenue minus COGS or COS—is a key number for most companies. It tells you the basic profitability of your product or service. If that part of your business is not profitable, your company is probably not going to survive long. After all, how can you expect to pay below-the-line expenses, including management salaries, if you aren't generating a healthy gross profit?

Profit

Profit is the amount left over after expenses are subtracted from revenue. There are three basic types of profit: gross profit, operating profit, and net profit. Each one is determined by subtracting certain categories of expenses from revenue.

But what does *healthy* mean? How much gross profit is enough? That varies substantially by industry, and it's likely to vary from one company to another even in the same industry. In the grocery business, gross profit is typically a small percentage of sales. In the jewelry business, it's typically a much larger percentage. Other things being equal, a company with larger revenues can thrive with a lower gross profit percentage than a smaller one. (That's one reason why Walmart can charge such low prices.) To gauge your company's gross profit, you can compare it with industry standards, particularly for companies of a similar size in your industry. You can also look at year-to-year trends, examining whether your gross profit is headed up or headed down. If it's headed down, you can ask why. Are production costs rising? Is your company discounting its sales? Understanding why gross profit is changing, if it is, helps managers figure out where to focus their attention.

Incidentally, though most income statements follow the format we described, a small but significant number of income statements put COGS or COS under a subhead called *operating expenses.* These income statements don't show a gross profit line at all. Microsoft is one company that uses this format. The lesson here? Pay close attention to the line items, and use

Gross Profit

Gross profit is sales minus cost of goods sold or cost of services. It is what is left over after a company has paid the direct costs incurred in making the product or delivering the service. Gross profit must be sufficient to cover a business's operating expenses, taxes, financing costs, and net profit.

your own financial intelligence to assess how a company has organized its expenses, and therefore how you should assess the profit lines.

Here too, however, you need to keep a sharp eye out for possible bias in the numbers. *Gross profit can be greatly affected by decisions about when to recognize revenue and by decisions about what to include in COGS.* Suppose you are HR director for a market research firm and you find that gross profit is headed downward. You look into the numbers, and at first it appears that service costs have gone up. So you and your team begin anticipating cuts in service costs, perhaps even including some layoffs. But when you do some more digging, you find that salaries that were previously in operating expenses have been moved into COGS. So service costs did not go up, and laying off people would be a mistake. Now you have to talk with the people in accounting. Why did they move those salaries? Why didn't they tell you? If those salaries are to remain in COGS, then maybe the firm's gross profit targets need to be reduced. But nothing else needs to change.

OPERATING PROFIT IS A KEY TO HEALTH

Operating profit—gross profit minus operating expenses or SG&A, including depreciation and amortization—is also known by the peculiar acronym EBIT (pronounced *EE-bit*). EBIT stands for earnings before interest and taxes. (Remember, *earnings* is just another name for profit). What has *not* yet been subtracted from revenue is interest and taxes. Why not? Because *operating profit is the profit a company earns from the business it is in*—from operations. Taxes don't really have anything to do with how well you are running your business. And interest expenses depend on whether the company is financed with debt or equity (we'll explain this difference

Operating Profit, or EBIT

Operating profit is gross profit minus operating expenses, which include depreciation and amortization. In other words, it shows the profit made from running the business.

in chapter 12). But the financial structure of the company doesn't say anything about how well it is run from an operational perspective.

So operating profit, or EBIT, is a good gauge of how well a company is being managed. It's watched closely by all stakeholders because it measures both overall demand for the company's products or services (sales) and the company's efficiency in delivering those products or services (costs). Bankers and investors look at operating profit to see whether the company will be able to pay its debts and earn money for its shareholders. Vendors look at it to see if the company will be able to pay its bills. (As we'll see later, however, operating profit is not always the best gauge of this.) Large customers examine operating profit to ascertain whether the company is doing an efficient job and is likely to be around for a while. Even savvy employees check out the operating profit figures. A healthy and growing operating profit suggests that the employees are going to be able to keep their jobs and may have opportunities for advancement.

However, remember that potential biases in the numbers can impact operating profit as well. Are there any one-time charges? What is the depreciation line? As we have seen, depreciation can be altered to affect profits one way or another. For a while, Wall Street analysts were watching companies' operating profit, or EBIT, closely. But some companies that were later revealed to have committed fraud turned out to be playing games with depreciation (remember Waste Management), so their EBIT numbers were suspect. Before long, Wall Street began focusing on another number—EBITDA (pronounced *EE-bid-dah*), or earnings before interest, taxes, depreciation, and amortization. Some people feel EBITDA is a better measure of a company's operating efficiency, because it ignores noncash charges such as depreciation altogether. (More recently, another number—free cash flow—has become the darling of Wall Street. You'll learn about it in the toolbox following part 4.)

NET PROFIT AND HOW TO FIX IT

Now, finally, let's get to the bottom line. Net profit. It is usually the last line on the income statement. Net profit is what is left over after everything is subtracted—cost of goods sold or cost of services, operating expenses, one-time charges, noncash expenses such as depreciation and amortiza-

Net Profit

Net profit is the bottom line of the income statement: what's left after *all* costs and expenses are subtracted from revenue. It's operating profit minus interest expenses, taxes, one-time charges, and any other costs not included in operating profit.

tion, interest, and taxes. When someone asks, "What's the bottom line?" he or she is almost always referring to net profit. Some of the key numbers used to measure a company, such as earnings per share and price/earnings ratio, are based on net profit. Yes, it is strange that they don't just call them profit per share and price/profit ratio. But they don't.

What if a company's net profit is lower than it ought to be? This can be a big issue, particularly because executives' bonuses may be tied to profit targets. On occasion, some decide to skirt accounting rules to improve the profit picture. Fannie Mae, for instance—the government-sponsored enterprise that plays a significant role in the US mortgage market—was charged with "extensive financial fraud" over the six-year period from 1998 to 2004. The goal of the fraud was to make it look as if earnings were right on target so that its executives would receive incentive payouts worth millions of dollars.[1]

Aside from monkeying with the books, there are only three possible fixes for low profitability. One, the company can increase profitable sales. This solution almost always requires a good deal of time. You have to find new markets or new prospects, work through the sales cycle, and so on. Two, it can figure out how to lower production costs and run more efficiently—that is, reduce COGS. This, too, takes time: you need to study the production process, find the inefficiencies, and implement changes. Three, it can cut operating expenses, which almost always means reducing the headcount. This is usually the only short-term solution available. That's why so many CEOs taking over troubled companies start by cutting the payroll in the overhead expense areas. It makes earnings look better fast.

Of course, layoffs can backfire. Morale suffers. Good people whom the new CEO wants to keep may begin looking for jobs elsewhere. And that's not the only danger. For example, "Chainsaw Al" Dunlap used the lay-people-off strategy a number of times to pump up the earnings of companies he took over, and Wall Street usually rewarded him for it. But the strategy didn't work when he got to Sunbeam. Yes, he slashed headcount, and yes, earnings rose. In fact, Wall Street was so enthusiastic about the company's pumped-up profitability that it bid Sunbeam's shares way up. But Dunlap's strategy all along had been to sell the company at a profit—and now, with its shares selling at a premium, the company was too expensive for prospective buyers to consider. Without a buyer, Sunbeam was forced to limp along until its problems became apparent and Chainsaw Al was forced out by the board.

The moral? For most companies, it's better to manage for the long haul and to focus on increasing profitable sales and reducing costs. Sure, operating expenses may have to be trimmed. But if that's your only focus, you're probably only postponing the day of reckoning.

CONTRIBUTION MARGIN—A DIFFERENT WAY OF LOOKING AT PROFIT

So far we have examined three different levels of profit—gross profit, operating profit, and net profit. All reflect the fact that an income statement is organized in a certain sequence: you begin with revenue, subtract COGS to get gross profit, subtract operating expenses to get operating profit, subtract taxes and interest and everything else to get net profit. If you categorized expenses differently, however, you would come up with a different measure of profit, and perhaps you could learn more about how well you are managing. That's the thinking behind a particular form of profit known as *contribution margin.*

Contribution Margin

Contribution margin indicates how much profit you are earning on the goods or services you sell, without accounting for your company's fixed costs. To calculate it, just subtract variable costs from sales.

Contribution margin is sales minus variable costs. It shows the profit you are earning on what you sell before you account for fixed costs. Remember what we discussed in chapter 8: variable costs are not the same as COGS or COS. So contribution margin is not the same as gross profit.

Here is what an income statement used for contribution margin analysis looks like:

CONTRIBUTION MARGIN ANALYSIS INCOME STATEMENT

Revenue
Variable costs
Contribution margin
Fixed costs
Operating profit
Interest/taxes
Net profit (loss)

Contribution margin shows you the aggregate amount of margin available after variable costs to cover fixed expenses and provide profit to the company. In effect, it shows you how much you must produce to cover your fixed costs.

Contribution margin analysis also helps managers compare products, make decisions about whether to add or subtract a product line, decide how to price a product or service, and even how to structure sales commissions. For example, a company should probably keep a product line with a positive contribution margin even if its conventionally calculated profit is negative. The contribution margin it generates helps pay for fixed costs. If its contribution margin is negative, however, the company loses money with each unit it produces. Since it can't make up that kind of loss with volume, it should either drop the product line or increase prices.

THE IMPACT OF EXCHANGE RATES ON PROFITABILITY

Sometimes operating managers have no control over factors that affect profit. An example is exchange rates—which, in our global economy, loom ever larger in many companies' calculations.

An exchange rate is just the price of one currency expressed in terms of another currency. An American visiting Hong Kong in autumn 2011, for example, could have bought about 7.8 Hong Kong dollars (HKD) for one US dollar. The price of those 7.8 HKD, in other words, is $1.00. However, exchange rates vary significantly over time. The fluctuations depend on trade flows, government budgets, relative interest rates, and a host of other variables.

Whenever a company from one country does business in another, the profitability of its operations will be affected by fluctuations in exchange rates. In the simplest case, imagine that a US manufacturer sells machines in Hong Kong for 780,000 HKD, or about $100,000 (in late 2011). Then suppose that the US dollar declines in value relative to the HKD—that is, you now need more than $1.00 to buy 7.8 HKD. Let's say the new rate is 6.8 HKD to the dollar. The manufacturer receives the same 780,000 HKD for its machines, but that money is now worth $114,706. Other things equal, those sales are 14.7 percent more profitable than they used to be. The manufacturer can pocket the difference, or it can decide to reduce prices to increase demand. The opposite will hold true, of course, if the US dollar increases in value relative to the HKD. In that case, people and companies who buy from Hong Kong will gain, and those who sell there will lose.

Many companies, of course, have highly complex overseas operations. They produce some products at home and some in foreign countries. They ship goods in both directions, and from one foreign country to another. Every international transaction involves some risk that exchange rates will fluctuate in the wrong direction, and that profits on the transaction will be less than expected.

Though operating managers can't do much about exchange rates themselves, the financial folks can and do take action to protect themselves against these risks, For example, they can purchase financial instruments that allow them to buy or sell certain currencies at predetermined prices, thus locking in exchange rates. This kind of hedge, as it is known in the financial world, helps protect against unexpected rate changes. Of course, hedges cost money, and they don't always work perfectly. So while a company can reduce the effects of exchange rates on profitability, it can rarely eliminate them.

Part Two
Toolbox

UNDERSTANDING VARIANCE

Variance just means difference. It might be the difference between budget and actual for the month or year, between actual this month and actual last month, and so on. It can be presented in dollars or percentages, or both. Percentages are usually more useful, because they provide a quick and easy basis of comparison between the two numbers.

The only difficulty with variance when you are reading a financial report lies in determining whether a variance is favorable or unfavorable. More revenue than expected, for instance, is favorable, while more expense than expected is unfavorable. Sometimes the folks in finance are helpful and let you know in a note that a variance enclosed in parentheses or a variance preceded by a minus sign is unfavorable. But often you have to figure it out on your own. We recommend doing a few calculations, figuring out whether the indicated variances are bad or good, then checking to see how they are displayed. Be sure to do the calculations for both a revenue line item and an expense line item. Sometimes parentheses or negative signs indicate the mathematical difference, not favorable or unfavorable. In that case, parentheses for a revenue line item might mean favorable, while parentheses for an expense line item might mean unfavorable.

PROFIT AT NONPROFITS

Nonprofit organizations use the same financial statements as for-profit companies, including the income statement. They also have a bottom line indicating the difference between revenue and expenses, just like for-profit companies. Sometimes the bottom line has a different label, but it is still a profit or a loss. And the fact is, a nonprofit organization needs to earn a profit. How can it survive over the long haul if it doesn't bring in more than it spends? It has to earn a surplus to invest in its future. The only difference is that a nonprofit can't distribute the profit to its owners, because it doesn't have owners. And of course it doesn't pay taxes. We often call nonprofits "nontaxed" organizations, which is really what they are.

Over the years, several nonprofits have hired our company to train their employees in finance. Why would a not-for-profit hire us to teach finance? The most common answer is that the organization is not making enough money to survive, and management wants to boost everyone's financial intelligence. It's just as important in this context as it is in the for-profit business world.

A QUICK REVIEW: "PERCENT OF" AND "PERCENT CHANGE"

Two common ways to analyze income statements are "percent of" and "percent change." Everybody learns these calculations in school, but you may have forgotten them. So take a quick look if you need to refresh your memory.

A *percent of* calculation tells you what percentage one figure is of another. For example, if you spent $60,000 on materials last year and the year's revenue was $500,000, you might want to know what percent of your revenue went for materials. The calculation is as follows:

$$\frac{\$60,000}{\$500,000} = 0.12 = 12\%$$

Percent change, in contrast, is the percentage by which a figure changed from one period to the next or from budget to actual. The formula for percent change from one year to the next is as follows:

$$\frac{\text{current year} - \text{prior year}}{\text{prior year}}$$

For example, if last year's revenue was $300,000 and this year's was $375,000, then the percent change is as follows:

$$\frac{\$375{,}000 - \$300{,}000}{\$300{,}000} = \frac{\$75{,}000}{\$300{,}000} = 0.25 = 25\%$$

Part Three

The Balance Sheet Reveals the Most

10

Understanding Balance Sheet Basics

THERE'S A PUZZLING FACT about financial statements. Maybe you've noticed it.

Give a company's financials to an experienced manager in the business, and the first thing he will turn to is the income statement. Most managers have—or aspire to have—"P&L responsibility." They're accountable for making the various forms of profit turn out right. They know that the income statement is where their performance is ultimately recorded. So that's what they look at first.

Now try giving the same set of financials to a banker, an experienced Wall Street investor, or maybe a veteran board member. The first statement this person will turn to is invariably the balance sheet. In fact, she's likely to pore over it for some time. Then she'll start flipping the pages, checking out the income statement and the cash flow statement—but always going back to the balance sheet.

Why don't managers do what the pros do? Why do they limit their attention to the income statement? We chalk it up to three factors:

- The balance sheet is a little harder to get your mind around than the income statement. Income statements, after all, are pretty intuitive. The balance sheet isn't—at least not until you understand the basics.

- Most companies' budgeting processes focus on revenue and expenses. In other words, the budget categories more or less align with the income statement. You can't be a manager without knowing something about budgeting—which automatically means that you're familiar with many of the lines on the income statement. Balance sheet data, by contrast, rarely figures in an operating manager's budgeting process (although the finance department certainly budgets the balance sheet accounts).

- *Managing* the balance sheet requires a deeper understanding of finance than managing an income statement. You not only have to know what the various categories refer to, you have to know how they fit together. You also have to understand how changes in the balance sheet affect the other financial statements, and vice versa.

Our guess is that you, too, are a bit wary of the balance sheet. But remember: what we're focusing on here is financial intelligence—understanding how financial results are measured and what you as a manager, an employee, or a leader can do to improve results. We won't get into the esoteric elements of the balance sheet, just the ones you need to appreciate the art of this statement and do the analyses that the statement makes possible.

SHOWING WHERE THINGS STAND RIGHT NOW

So what is the balance sheet? *It's no more, and no less, than a statement of what a business owns and what it owes at a particular point in time.* The difference between what a company owns and what it owes represents *equity.* Just as one of a company's goals is to increase profitability, another is to increase equity. And as it happens, the two are intimately related.

What is this relationship? Consider an analogy. Profitability is sort of like the grade you receive for a course in college. You spend a semester writing papers and taking exams. At the end of the semester, the instructor tallies your performance and gives you an A– or a C+ or whatever. Equity is more like your overall grade point average (GPA). Your GPA always reflects your cumulative performance, but at only one point in time. Any one grade affects it, but doesn't determine it. The income statement affects the

Equity

Equity is the shareholders' "stake" in the company as measured by accounting rules. It's also called the company's book value. In accounting terms, equity is always assets minus liabilities; it is also the sum of all capital paid in by shareholders *plus* any profits earned by the company since its inception *minus* dividends paid out to shareholders. That's the accounting formula, anyway. Remember that what a company's shares are actually worth is whatever a willing buyer will pay for them.

balance sheet much the way an individual grade affects your GPA. Make a profit in any given period, and the equity on your balance sheet will show an increase. Lose money, and it will show a decrease. Over time, the equity section of the balance sheet shows the *accumulation* of profits or losses left in the business; the line is called retained earnings or sometimes accumulated earnings. If the company has built up a net loss over time, then the balance sheet will show a negative number called accumulated deficit in this section of the balance sheet.

Here, too, however, understanding the balance sheet means understanding all the assumptions, decisions, and estimates that go into it. Like the income statement, the balance sheet is in many respects a work of art, not just a work of calculation.

INDIVIDUALS AND BUSINESSES

Since the balance sheet is so important, we want to begin with some simple lessons. Bear with us—it's important in this case to crawl before you walk.

Start by considering an individual's financial situation, or financial worth, again at a given point in time. You add up what the person owns, subtract what she owes, and come up with her *net worth*:

owns – owes = net worth

Another way to state the same thing is this:

owns = owes + net worth

For an individual, the ownership category might include cash in the bank, big-ticket items like a house and a car, and all the other property the person can lay claim to. It also would include financial assets such as stocks and bonds or a retirement account. The "owing" category includes mortgage, car loan, credit card balances, and any other debt. Note that we're avoiding for the moment the question of *how* to calculate some of those numbers. What's the value of the house—what the person paid for it or what it might bring today? How about the car or the TV? You can see the art of finance peeking around the curtain here—but more on that in a moment.

Now move from an individual to a business. Same concepts, different language:

- What the company owns is called its *assets.*
- What it owes is called its *liabilities.*
- What it's worth is called *owners' equity* or *shareholders' equity.*

And the basic equation now looks like this:

assets – liabilities = owners' equity

or this:

assets = liabilities + owners' equity

The latter formulation is one you might recognize from your Accounting 101 class years ago. It is the classic equation of the balance sheet. The instructor probably called it the *fundamental accounting equation.* You also learned that it reflects the two sides of the balance sheet: assets on the one side, liabilities and owners' equity on the other. The sum on one side has to equal the sum on the other side; the balance sheet has to balance. Before you finish this part of the book, you will understand why.

READING A BALANCE SHEET

First, however, find a sample balance sheet, either your own company's or one in an annual report. (Or just look at the sample in the appendix.) Since the balance sheet shows the company's financial situation at a given point in time, there should be a specific date at the top. It's usually the end of a month, quarter, year, or fiscal year. When you're looking at financial statements together, you typically want to see an income statement for a month, quarter, or year, along with the balance sheet for the end of the period reported. Unlike income statements, balance sheets are almost always for an entire organization. Sometimes a large corporation creates subsidiary balance sheets for its operating divisions, but it rarely does so for a single facility. As we'll see, accounting professionals have to do some estimating on the balance sheet, just the way they do with the income statement. Remember the delivery business we described when we were discussing depreciation in chapter 8? The way you depreciate the truck affects not only the income statement but also the value of assets shown on the balance sheet. It turns out that most of the assumptions and biases in the income statement flow into the balance sheet one way or another.

Balance sheets come in two typical formats. The traditional model shows assets on the left-hand side of the page and liabilities and owners' equity on the right-hand side, with liabilities at the top. The less traditional format puts assets on top, liabilities in the middle, and owners' equity on the bottom. Whatever the format, the "balance" remains the same: assets must equal liabilities plus owners' equity. (In the nonprofit world, where organizations do not have shareholders, owners' equity is sometimes called "net assets.") Often a balance sheet shows comparative figures for, say, December 31 of the most recent year and December 31 of the previous year. Check the column headings to see what points in time are being compared.

Fiscal Year

A fiscal year is any twelve-month period that a company uses for accounting purposes. Many companies use the calendar year, but some use other periods (October 1 to September 30, for example). Some retailers use a specific weekend, such as the last Sunday of the year, to mark the end of their fiscal year. You must know the company's fiscal year to ascertain how recent the information you are looking at is.

As with income statements, some organizations have unusual line items on their balance sheets that you won't find discussed in this book. Remember, many of these items may be clarified in the footnotes. In fact, balance sheets are notorious for their footnotes. Coca-Cola's 2010 annual report, for example, contained sixty-one pages of notes, many of them pertaining to the balance sheet. Companies often include a standard disclaimer in the notes making the very point about the art of finance that we are making in this book. Coca-Cola, for instance, says:

Management of the Company is responsible for the preparation and integrity of the consolidated financial statements appearing in our annual report on Form 10-K. The financial statements were prepared in conformity with generally accepted accounting principles appropriate in the circumstances and, accordingly, include certain amounts based on our best judgments and estimates. Financial information in this annual report on Form 10-K is consistent with that in the financial statements.

If the notes don't provide the necessary enlightenment, you can leave the items to the financial professionals. (If something you're wondering about is significant, though, it makes sense to ask someone in your finance organization about the item and the number that goes with it.)

Since the balance sheet is new to most managers, we want to walk you through the most common line items. Some may look strange at first, but don't worry: just keep in mind that distinction between "owned" and "owed." As with the income statement, we'll pause along the way to see which lines are most easily monkeyed with.

11

Assets

More Estimates and Assumptions (Except for Cash)

ASSETS ARE WHAT THE COMPANY OWNS: cash and securities, machinery and equipment, buildings and land, whatever. *Current assets,* which usually come first on the balance sheet in the United States, include anything that can be turned into cash in less than a year. *Long-term* assets include physical assets that have a useful life of more than a year—usually anything that is either depreciated or amortized. They can also include land, goodwill, and long-term investments, none of which are depreciated.

TYPES OF ASSETS

Within those broad categories, of course, are many line items. We'll list the most common ones—those that appear on nearly every company's balance sheet.

Cash and Cash Equivalents

This is the hard stuff. Money in the bank. Money in money-market accounts. Also publicly traded stocks and bonds—the kind you can turn into cash in a day or less if you need to. Another name for this category is *liquid assets.* This is one of the few line items that are not subject to accountants' discretion. When Microsoft says it has $56 billion in cash and short-term investments, or whatever the latest number is, it means it really has that much in banks, money funds, and publicly traded securities. Of course, companies can lie. In 2003, the giant Italian company Parmalat reported on its balance sheet that it had billions in an account with Bank of America. It didn't. In 2009, the CEO of a large Indian outsourcing company, Satyam Computer Services, acknowledged that he had "inflated the amount of cash on the balance sheet . . . by nearly $1 billion."[1]

Accounts Receivable, or A/R

This is the amount customers owe the company. Remember, revenue is a promise to pay, so accounts receivable includes all the promises that haven't yet been collected. Why is this an asset? Because all or most of these commitments will convert to cash and soon *will* belong to the company. It's like a loan from the company to its customers—and the company owns the customers' obligation. Accounts receivable is one line item that managers need to watch closely, particularly since investors, analysts, and creditors are likely to be watching it as well. We'll say more on how to manage accounts receivable in part 7, where we discuss working capital.

Sometimes a balance sheet includes an item labeled "allowance for bad debt" that is subtracted from accounts receivable. This is the accountants' estimate—usually based on past experience—of the dollars owed by customers who don't pay their bills. In many companies, subtracting a bad-debt allowance provides a more accurate reflection of the value of those accounts receivable. But note well: estimates are already creeping in. In fact,

"Smoothing" Earnings

You might think that Wall Street would like a big spike in a company's profits—more money for shareholders, right? But if the spike is unforeseen and unexplained—and especially if it catches Wall Street by surprise—investors are likely to react negatively, taking it as a sign that management isn't in control of the business. So companies like to "smooth" their earnings, maintaining steady and predictable growth.

many companies use the bad-debt reserve as a tool to "smooth" their earnings. When you increase the bad-debt reserve on the balance sheet, you have to record an expense against profit on the income statement. That lowers your reported earnings. When you *decrease* a reserve for bad debt, similarly, the adjustment increases profit on the income statement. Since the bad-debt reserve is always an estimate, there is room here for subjectivity.

Inventory

Service companies typically don't have much in the way of inventory, but nearly every other company—manufacturers, wholesalers, retailers—does. One part of the inventory figure is the value of the products that are ready to be sold. That's called *finished goods* inventory. A second part, usually relevant only to manufacturers, is the value of products that are under construction. Accountants dub that *work-in-process* inventory, or just WIP (pronounced *whip*). Then, of course, there's the inventory of raw materials that will be used to make products. That's called—stand back—*raw materials* inventory.

Accountants can (and do!) spend days on end talking about ways of valuing inventory. We plan to spend no time at all, because it doesn't really affect most managers' jobs. (If your job is inventory management, of course, the accountants' discussion affects you greatly—and you should find a book on the topic.) However, different methods of inventory valuation can often alter the assets side of a balance sheet significantly. If the company changes its method of valuing inventory during a given year, that fact should appear in a footnote to the balance sheet. Many companies detail how they accounted for their inventories in the footnotes, as Barnes & Noble did in one recent annual report:

> *Merchandise inventories are stated at the lower of cost or market. Cost is determined primarily by the retail inventory method under both the first-in, first-out (FIFO) basis and the last-in, first-out (LIFO) basis. The Company uses the retail inventory method for 97% of the Company's merchandise inventories. As of April 30, 2011, and May 1, 2010, 87% of the Company's inventory on the retail inventory method was valued under the FIFO basis. B&N College's textbook and trade book inventories are valued using the LIFO method, where the related reserve was not*

material to the recorded amount of the Company's inventories or results of operations.

What you do need to remember as a manager, however, is that *all* inventory costs money. It is created at the expense of cash. (Maybe you've heard the expression "All our cash is tied up in inventory," though we hope you don't hear it too often.) In fact, this is one way companies can improve their cash position. Decrease your inventory, other things being equal, and you raise your company's cash level. A company always wants to carry as little inventory as possible, provided that it still has materials ready for its manufacturing processes and products ready when customers come calling. We'll come back to this topic later in the book.

Property, Plant, and Equipment (PPE)

This line on the balance sheet includes buildings, machinery, trucks, computers, and every other physical asset a company owns. The PPE figure is the total number of dollars it cost to buy all the facilities and equipment the company uses to operate the business. Note that the relevant cost here is the *purchase price*. Without constant appraisals, nobody really knows how much a company's real estate or equipment might be worth on the open market. So accountants, governed by the principle of conservatism, say in effect, "Let's use what we do know, which is the cost of acquiring those assets."

Another reason for using purchase price is to avoid more opportunities to bias the numbers. Suppose an asset—land, for example—has actually increased in value. If we wanted to "mark it up" on the balance sheet to its current value, we would have to record a profit on the income statement. But that profit would be based simply on someone's opinion as to what the land was worth today. This is not a good idea. Some companies go so far as to set up corporate shells, often owned by a company executive or other insider, and then sell assets to those shells. That allows them to record a profit, just the way they would if they were selling off assets. But it is not the kind of profit an investor or the Securities and Exchange Commission likes to see.

Later in this chapter we will discuss *mark-to-market* accounting, which requires companies to value certain kinds of assets at their current market value. For the moment, just remember that the basis for valuing most assets is their purchase price. Of course, the fact that companies rely on purchase price to value their assets can create some striking anomalies. Maybe you work for an entertainment company that bought land around Los Angeles for $500,000 thirty years ago. The land could be worth $5 million today—but it will still be valued at $500,000 on the balance sheet. Sophisticated investors like to nose around in companies' balance sheets in hopes of finding such undervalued assets.

Less: Accumulated Depreciation

Land doesn't wear out, so accountants don't record any depreciation each year. But buildings and equipment do. The point of accounting depreciation, however, isn't to estimate what the buildings and equipment are worth right now; the point is to allocate the investment in the asset over the time it is used to generate revenue and profit (remember the matching principle discussed in chapter 5). The depreciation charge is a way of ensuring that the income statement accurately reflects the true cost of producing goods or delivering services. To calculate *accumulated* depreciation, accountants simply add up all the charges for depreciation they have taken since the day an asset was bought.

We showed you in chapter 8 how a company can "magically" go from unprofitable to profitable just by changing the way it depreciates its assets. That art-of-finance magic extends to the balance sheet as well. If a company decides its trucks can last six years rather than three, it will record a 50 percent smaller charge on its income statement year after year. That means less accumulated depreciation on the balance sheet, a higher figure for net PPE, and thus more assets. More assets, by the fundamental accounting equation, translates into more owners' equity in the form of retained earnings.

Goodwill

Goodwill is found on the balance sheets of companies that have acquired other companies. It's the difference between what a company paid for another company and what the physical assets of the acquired company are worth.

OK, that was a mouthful. But it isn't as complex as it sounds. Say you're the CEO of a company that is out shopping, and you spot a nice little

Acquisitions

An acquisition occurs when one company buys another. Often you'll see in the newspaper the words *merger* or *consolidation*. Don't be fooled: one company still bought the other. They just use a more neutral-sounding term to make the deal look better.

warehousing business called MJQ Storage that fits your needs perfectly. You agree to buy MJQ for $5 million. By the rules of accounting, if you pay cash, the asset called cash on your balance sheet will decrease by $5 million. That means other assets have to rise by $5 million. After all, the balance sheet still has to balance. And you haven't done anything so far that would change liabilities or owners' equity.

Now, watch closely. Since you are buying a collection of physical assets (among other things), you will appraise those assets the way any buyer would. Maybe you find that MJQ's buildings, shelving, forklifts, and computers are worth $2 million. That doesn't mean you made a bad deal. You are buying a going concern with a name, talented and knowledgeable employees, and so on, and these so-called intangibles can in some cases be much *more* valuable than the tangible assets. (How much would you pay for the brand name Coca-Cola? Or for Dell Computer's customer list?) In our example, you're buying $3 million worth of intangibles. Accountants

Intangibles

A company's intangible assets include anything that has value but that you can't touch or spend: employees' skills, customer lists, proprietary knowledge, patents, brand names, reputation, strategic strengths, and so on. Most of these assets are not found on the balance sheet unless an acquiring company pays for them and records them as goodwill. The exception is intellectual property, such as patents and copyrights. This can be shown on the balance sheet and amortized over its useful life.

call that $3 million "goodwill." The $3 million of goodwill and the $2 million of physical assets add up to the $5 million you paid and the corresponding $5 million increase in assets on the balance sheet.

And now we want to tell a little story about goodwill; it shows the art of finance at work.

In years past, goodwill was amortized. (Remember, amortization is the same idea as depreciation, except that it applies to intangible assets.) Assets were typically depreciated over two to five years, but goodwill was amortized over thirty years. That was the rule.

Then the rule changed. The people who write those generally accepted accounting principles—the Financial Accounting Standards Board, or FASB—decided that if goodwill consists of the reputation, the customer base, and so on of the company you are buying, then all those assets don't lose value over time. They actually may become *more* valuable over time. In short, goodwill is more like land than it is like equipment. So not amortizing it helps accountants portray that accurate reflection of reality that they are always seeking.

But look at the effect. When you bought MJQ Storage, you wound up with $3 million worth of goodwill on your balance sheet. Before the rule change, you would have amortized the goodwill over thirty years at $100,000 per year. In other words, you would have deducted $100,000 a year from revenue, thereby reducing the profitability of your company by the same amount. Meanwhile, you're depreciating MJQ's physical assets (worth $2 million) over, say, a four-year period at $500,000 per year. Again, that $500,000 would be subtracted from revenue to determine profit.

So what happens? Before the rule change, other things being equal, you wanted to have *more* goodwill and *less* in physical assets, simply because goodwill is amortized over a longer period of time, so the amount subtracted from revenue to determine profit is less (keeping profits higher). You had an incentive to shop for companies where most of what you'd be buying was goodwill, and you had an incentive to *undervalue* the physical assets of the company you were buying. (Remember, it is often your own people who are doing the appraisal of those assets!)

Today, goodwill sits on the books and isn't amortized. Now nothing at all is subtracted from revenue, and profitability is correspondingly higher. You have an even bigger incentive to look for companies without much in the way of physical assets, and even more of an incentive to undervalue those assets. Tyco was one company that was accused of taking advantage of this rule. Several years ago, as we noted earlier, Tyco was buying companies at breakneck speed—more than six hundred in two years' time. Many analysts felt that Tyco regularly undervalued the assets of these numerous companies. Doing so would increase the goodwill included in all those acquisitions and lower the depreciation Tyco had to take each year. That, in turn, would make profit higher and in theory would drive up Tyco's share price.

But eventually, analysts and investors noticed a fact that we alluded to in part 1, namely that Tyco had too much goodwill on its books and too little (relatively speaking) in the way of physical assets. They began focusing on a measure called *tangible net worth*, which is just total assets minus intangible assets minus liabilities. When this metric turns negative, investors tend to get nervous and often sell their stock.

Intellectual Property, Patents, and Other Intangibles

How do you account for the cost of creating a new software program that you expect to generate revenue for years? What about the cost of developing a new wonder drug, which is protected by a twenty-year patent (from the date of application)? Obviously, it makes no sense to record the whole cost as an expense on the income statement in any given period, any more than you would record the whole cost of buying a truck. Like a truck, the software and the patent will help generate revenue in future accounting periods. So these investments are considered intangible assets and should be amortized over the life of the revenue stream they generate. By the same token, however, R&D expenses that do *not* result in an asset likely to generate revenue should be recorded as an expense on the income statement.

You can see the potential for subjectivity here. Some software companies, for example, are famous for spending considerable sums on R&D, then amortizing those sums over time, thus making their profits look higher. Others choose to expense R&D as it is incurred—a more conservative approach. Amortization is fine if the R&D is actually expected to generate revenue, but not if it isn't. Computer Associates is one company that got itself into trouble for amortizing R&D on products that had a questionable future. But even when there is no question of fraud, you need to know how aggressive or conservative your company's policies and practices on amortization are. Like depreciation, amortization decisions can often have a sizable effect on profitability and owners' equity.

Accruals and Prepaid Assets

To explain this line item, let's look at a hypothetical example. Say you start a bicycle manufacturing company, and you rent manufacturing space for the entire year for $60,000. Since your company is a lousy credit risk—nobody likes to do business with a start-up for just this reason—the landlord insists on payment up front.

Now, we know from the matching principle that it doesn't make sense to "book" the entire $60,000 in January as an expense on the income statement. It's rent for the whole year, and it has to be spread out over all twelve months. So in January you put $5,000 on the income statement for rent. But where does the other $55,000 go? You have to keep track of it somewhere. Well, prepaid rent is one example of a prepaid asset. You have bought something—you own the rights to that space for a year—so it is an asset. And you keep track of assets on the balance sheet.

Every month, of course, you'll have to move $5,000 out of the prepaid-asset line on the balance sheet and put it in the income statement as an expense for rent. That's called an accrual, and the "account" on the balance sheet that records what has not yet been expensed is called an accrued asset account. Though the terms are confusing, note that the practice is still conservative: we're keeping track of all our known expenses, and we're also tracking what we paid for in advance.

But the art of finance can creep in here as well, because there is room for judgment on what to accrue and what to charge in any given period. Say, for example, your company is developing a major advertising campaign. The work is all done in January, and it comes to $1 million. The accountants might decide that this campaign will benefit the company for two years, so they would book the $1 million as a prepaid asset and charge one-twenty-fourth of the cost each month on the income statement. A company facing a tough month is likely to decide that this is the best course—after all, it's better to deduct one-twenty-fourth of a million dollars from profits than the whole million. But what if January is a great month? Then the company might decide to "expense" the entire campaign—charge it all against January's revenue—because, well, they aren't *sure* that it will help generate revenue during the next two years. Now they have an advertising campaign that's all paid for, and profits in the months to come will be correspondingly higher. In a perfect world, our accounting friends would have a crystal ball to tell them exactly how long that advertising campaign will generate revenue. Since they don't yet have such a device, they must rely on estimates.

VALUING ASSETS: THE MARK-TO-MARKET RULE

Though most assets are valued at purchase price less accumulated depreciation, there is one exception to this approach. It's known as the *mark-to-market rule*, and use of the rule is often called *mark-to-market accounting*. The rule allows (and in some cases requires) certain classes of assets to be listed at their current market value. To qualify for this kind of treatment, assets must meet two criteria. One, their value must be able to be determined without an appraisal. Two, they must be held by the company as short-term investments.

Publicly traded financial assets such as stocks and bonds, whose value is determined every day in the public markets, may meet these two criteria. Imagine, for instance, that Amalgamated Services has a spare $100 million dollars in cash on its balance sheet and chooses to buy 1 million shares of IBM at $100 a share. Amalgamated lists its new current asset on the balance sheet as "stock $100 million." Three months later, the IBM stock is trading at $110. Amalgamated now marks the 1 million shares up to $110 million and records a gain of $10 million on its income statement (typically in the line labeled "other income"). Of course, if the stock is at $95 after three months, then Amalgamated's stock holding must be marked down to $95 million, and it must record a loss of $5 million in the income statement. Unlike in conventional accounting, Amalgamated records these gains or losses while it is still holding the stock. So mark-to-market accounting gains or losses take place purely on paper.

The financial crisis of 2008 revealed two issues surrounding this rule that can have serious consequences in the capital markets. First, how does one determine whether a certain group of assets is held for sale or held as a long-term investment? Two businesses could have the same assets, one designating them as buy-and-sell and thus marking them to market, the other planning to hold the assets and thus valuing them at cost. It seems strange that the same assets can be presented differently, depending on an organization's intentions. Second, what happens when the market nearly collapses or fails outright? In the toolbox following this part, we'll see what happened when hundreds of financial institutions were forced to mark their loan assets to market. The financial crisis was in many ways a mark-to-market crisis, as we explain in the toolbox. But if the crisis eases and the institution then chooses to hold the assets until the market recovers, must it still take the mark-to-market losses? This is a question that is still under debate.

That's it for assets. Add them all up, along with whatever extraneous items you might find, and you get the "total assets" line at the bottom of the left side. Now it's time to move on to the other side—liabilities and owners' equity.

12

On the Other Side

Liabilities and Equity

WE SAID EARLIER THAT LIABILITIES are what a company owes and equity is its net worth. There's another—only slightly different—way to look at this side of the balance sheet, which is that *it shows how the assets were obtained.* If a company borrows funds in any way, shape, or form to obtain an asset, the borrowing is going to show up on one or another of the liabilities lines. If it sells stock to obtain an asset, that will be reflected on one of the lines under owners' equity.

TYPES OF LIABILITIES

But first things first, which on this side of the balance sheet means liabilities, the financial obligations a company owes to other entities. Liabilities are always divided into two main categories. *Current* liabilities are those that have to be paid off in less than a year. *Long-term* liabilities are those that come due over a longer time frame. Liabilities are usually listed on the balance sheet from shortest-term to longest-term, so the very layout tells you something about what's due when.

Current Portion of Long-Term Debt

If your company owes $100,000 to a bank on a long-term loan, maybe $10,000 of it is due this year. So that's the amount that shows up in the current liabilities section of the balance sheet. The line will be labeled "current portion of long-term debt" or something like that. The other $90,000 shows up under long-term liabilities.

Short-Term Loans

These are lines of credit and short-term revolving loans. These short-term credit lines are usually secured by current assets such as accounts receivable and inventory. The entire balance outstanding is shown here.

Accounts Payable

Accounts payable shows the amount the company owes its vendors. The company receives goods and services from suppliers every day and typically doesn't pay their bills for at least thirty days. The vendors, in effect, have loaned the company money. Accounts payable shows how much was owed on the date of the balance sheet. Any balance on a company's credit cards is usually included in accounts payable.

Accrued Expenses and Other Short-Term Liabilities

This catch-all category includes everything else the company owes. One example is payroll. Let's assume that you get paid on October 1. Does it make sense to charge your pay as an expense on the income statement in October? Probably not—your October paycheck is for work performed in September. So the accountants would figure out or estimate how much the company owes you on October 1 for work completed in September and then charge those expenses to September. This is an accrued liability. It's like an internal bill in September for a payment to be made in October. Accrued liabilities are part of the matching principle—we have matched expenses with the revenue they help to bring in every month.

Deferred Revenue

Some companies have an item called *deferred revenue* on their balance sheets. This is puzzling to the financial novice: how can revenue be a liability? Well, a liability is a financial obligation the company owes to others. Deferred revenue represents money received for products or services that have not yet been delivered. So it's an obligation. Once the product or service has been delivered, the corresponding revenue will be included in the top line of the income statement, and it will come off the balance sheet. Industries where you might see deferred revenue on the balance sheet include airlines (you pay before you fly) and project-based businesses (a client typically makes a down payment prior to the start of the work). This method of dealing with revenue not yet earned is in line with the principle of conservatism: don't recognize gains until they are actually earned.

Long-Term Liabilities

Most long-term liabilities are loans. But there are also other liabilities that you might see listed here. Examples include deferred bonuses or compensation, deferred taxes, and pension liabilities. If these other liabilities are substantial, this section of the balance sheet needs to be watched closely.

OWNERS' EQUITY

Finally! Remember the equation? Owners' equity is what's left after we subtract liabilities from assets. Equity includes the capital provided by investors and the profits retained by the company over time. Owners' equity goes by many names, including shareholders' equity and stockholders' equity. The owners' equity line items listed in some companies' balance sheets

Capital

The word means a number of things in business. *Physical* capital is plant, equipment, vehicles, and the like. *Financial* capital from an investor's point of view is the stocks and bonds he holds; from a company's point of view it is the shareholders' equity investment plus whatever funds the company has borrowed. "Sources of capital" in an annual report shows where the company got its money. "Uses of capital" shows how the company used its money.

can be quite detailed and confusing. They typically include the following categories.

Preferred Shares

Preferred shares—also known as preference stock or shares—are a specific type of stock. People who hold preferred shares usually receive dividends on their investment before the holders of common stock get a nickel. But preferred shares typically carry a fixed dividend, so their price doesn't fluctuate as much as the price of common shares. Investors who hold preferred shares may not receive the full benefit of a company's growth in value. When the company issues preferred shares, it sells them to investors at a certain initial price. The value shown on the balance sheet reflects that price.

Most preferred shares do not carry voting rights. In a way, they're more like bonds than like common stock. The difference? With a bond, the owner gets a fixed coupon or interest payment, and with preferred shares the owner gets a fixed dividend. Companies use preferred stock to raise money because it does not carry the same legal implications as debt. If a company cannot pay a coupon on a bond, bondholders can force it into bankruptcy. Holders of preferred shares normally can't.

Common Shares or Common Stock

Unlike most preferred shares, common shares usually carry voting rights. People who hold them can vote for members of the board of directors (usually one share, one vote) and on any other matter that may be put before the shareholders. Common shares may or may not pay dividends. The value shown on the balance sheet is based on the issuing price of the shares; it's shown as "par value" and "paid-in capital."

Dividends

Dividends are funds distributed to shareholders taken from a company's equity. In public companies, dividends are typically distributed at the end of a quarter or year.

Retained Earnings

Retained earnings or accumulated earnings are the profits that have been reinvested in the business instead of being paid out in dividends. The number represents the *total* after-tax income that has been reinvested or retained over the life of the business. Sometimes a company that holds a lot of retained earnings in the form of cash—Microsoft is an example—comes under pressure to pay out some of the money to shareholders, in the form of dividends. After all, what shareholder wants to see his money just sitting there in the company's coffers, rather than being reinvested in productive assets? Of course, you may see an accumulated deficit—a negative number—which indicates that the company has lost money over time.

So owners' equity is what the shareholders would receive if the company were sold, right? Of course not! Remember all those rules, estimates, and assumptions that affect the balance sheet. Assets are recorded at their acquisition price less accumulated depreciation. Goodwill is piled up with every acquisition the company makes, and it is never amortized. And of course the company has intangible assets of its own, such as its brand name and customer list, which don't show up on the balance sheet at all. Moral: the market value of a company almost *never* matches its equity or book value on the balance sheet. The actual market value of a company is what a willing buyer would pay for it. In the case of a public company, that value is estimated by calculating the company's market cap, or the number of shares outstanding times the share price on any given day. In the case of private companies, the market value can be estimated by one of the valuation methods described in part 1.

13

Why the Balance Sheet Balances

IF YOU LEARNED IN SCHOOL about the fundamental accounting equation, the instructor probably said something like this: "It's called the balance sheet because it *balances*. Assets *always* equal liabilities plus owners' equity." But even if you dutifully wrote down that answer on the exam, you may be less than 100 percent crystal-clear on why the balance sheet balances. So here are three ways of understanding it.

REASONS FOR BALANCE

First, let's go back to an individual. You can look at a company's balance sheet just the same way you'd look at a person's net worth. Net worth *has* to equal what he owns minus what he owes, because that's the way we define the term. The first formulation of the "individual" equation in chapter 10 is *owns – owes = net worth.* It's the same for a business. Owners' equity is defined as assets minus liabilities.

Second, look at what the balance sheet shows. On one side are the assets, which is what the company owns. On the other side are the liabilities and equity, which show how the company obtained what it owns. Since you can't get something for nothing, the "owns" side and the "how we obtained it" side will always be in balance. They have to be.

Third, consider what happens to the balance sheet over time. This approach should help you see why it always *stays* in balance.

Imagine a company that is just starting out. Its owner has invested $50,000 in the business, so he has $50,000 in cash on the assets side of the balance sheet. He has no liabilities yet, so he has $50,000 in owners' equity. The balance sheet balances.

Now, the company buys a truck for $36,000 in cash. If nothing else changes—and if you constructed a balance sheet right after the truck transaction—the assets side of the balance sheet would look like this:

Assets	
Cash	$14,000
Property, plant, and equipment	36,000

It still adds up to $50,000—and on the other side of the balance sheet, he still has $50,000 worth of owners' equity. The balance sheet still balances.

Next, imagine that the owner decides he needs more cash. So he goes to the bank and borrows $10,000, raising his total cash to $24,000. Now the balance sheet looks like this:

Assets	
Cash	$24,000
Property, plant, and equipment	36,000

Now it adds up to $60,000. He has increased his assets. But of course, he has increased his liabilities as well. So the other side of the balance sheet looks like this:

Liabilities and Owners' Equity	
Bank loan	$10,000
Owners' equity	$50,000

That, too, adds up to $60,000.

Note that owners' equity remains unchanged throughout all these transactions. Owners' equity is affected *only* when a company takes in funds from its owners, pays out money to its owners, or records a profit or loss.

In the meantime, *every transaction that affects one side of the balance sheet affects the other as well.* For example:

- A company uses $100,000 cash to pay off a loan. The cash line on the assets side decreases by $100,000, and the liabilities line on the other side decreases by the same amount. So the balance sheet stays in balance.
- A company buys a $100,000 machine, paying $50,000 down and owing the rest. Now the cash line is $50,000 less than it used to be—but the new machine shows up on the assets side at $100,000. So total assets increase by $50,000. Meanwhile, the $50,000 owed on the machine shows up on the liabilities side. Again, we're still in balance.

As long as you remember the fundamental fact that transactions affect both sides of the balance sheet, you'll be OK. That's why the balance sheet balances. Understanding this point is a basic building block of financial intelligence. Remember, if assets don't equal liabilities and equity, you do not have a balance sheet.

14

The Income Statement Affects the Balance Sheet

SO FAR WE HAVE BEEN CONSIDERING the balance sheet by itself. But here's one of the best-kept secrets in the world of financial statements: *a change in one statement nearly always has an impact on the other statements.* So when you're managing the income statement, you're also having an effect on the balance sheet.

PROFITS AND EQUITY

To see the relationship between profit, from the income statement, and equity, which appears on the balance sheet, we'll look at a couple of examples. Here's a highly simplified balance sheet for a brand-new (and very small!) company:

Assets	
Cash	$25
Accounts receivable	0
Total assets	$25

Liabilities and Owners' Equity	
Accounts payable	$ 0
Owners' equity	$25

Say we operate this company for a month. We buy $50 worth of parts and materials, which we use to produce and sell $100 worth of finished product. We also incur $25 in other expenses. The income statement for the month looks like this:

Sales	$100
Cost of goods sold	50
Gross profit	50
All expenses	25
Net profit	$ 25

Now: what has changed on the balance sheet?

- First, we have spent all our cash to cover expenses.
- Second, we have $100 in receivables from our customers.
- Third, we have incurred $50 in obligations to our suppliers.

Thus the balance sheet at the end of the month looks like this:

Assets	
Cash	$ 0
Accounts receivable	100
Total assets	$100

Liabilities and Owners' Equity	
Accounts payable	$ 50
Owners' equity	$ 50
Liabilities and owners' equity	$100

As you can see, that $25 of net income becomes $25 of owners' equity. On a more detailed balance sheet, it would appear under owners' equity as retained earnings. That's true in any business: net profit adds to equity unless it is paid out in dividends. By the same token, a net loss decreases equity. If a business loses money every month, liabilities will eventually exceed assets, creating negative equity. Then it is a candidate for bankruptcy court.

Note something else about this simple example: the company wound up that month with no cash! It was making money, and equity was growing, but it had nothing in the bank. So a good manager needs to be aware of how both cash and profits interact on the balance sheet. This is a topic we'll return to in part 4, when we take up the cash flow statement.

AND MANY OTHER EFFECTS

The relationship between profits and equity isn't the only link between changes in the income statement and changes on the balance sheet. Far from it. Every sale recorded on the income statement generates an increase either in cash (if it's a cash sale) or in receivables. Every payroll dollar recorded under COGS or under operating expenses represents a dollar less on the cash line or a dollar more on the accrued expenses line of the balance sheet. A purchase of materials adds to accounts payable, and so on. And of course, all these changes have an effect on total assets or liabilities.

Overall, if a manager's job is to boost profitability, he or she can have a positive effect on the balance sheet, just because profits increase equity. But it isn't quite so simple, because it matters *how* the company earns those profits, and it matters what happens to the other assets and liabilities on the balance sheet itself. For example:

- A plant manager hears of a good deal on an important raw material and asks the purchasing department to buy a lot of it. Makes sense, right? Not necessarily. The inventory line on the balance sheet increases. The accounts payable line increases a corresponding amount. Eventually, the company will have to draw down its cash to cover the accounts payable—possibly long before the material is used to generate revenue. Meanwhile, the company has to pay for warehousing the inventory, and it may need to borrow money to cover the decrease in cash. Figuring out whether to take advantage of the deal requires detailed analysis; be sure to consider all of the financial issues when making such decisions.

- A sales manager is looking to boost revenue and profit, and decides to target smaller businesses as customers. Is it a good idea? Maybe not. Smaller customers may not be as good credit risks as larger ones. Accounts receivable may rise disproportionately because the customers are slower to pay. The accountants may need to increase that "bad debt" allowance, which reduces profit, assets, and thus equity. The financially intelligent sales manager will need to investigate pricing possibilities: can he increase gross margin to compensate for the increased risk on sales to smaller customers?

- An IT manager makes a decision to buy a new computer system, believing that the new system will boost productivity and therefore contribute to profitability. But how is the new equipment going to be paid for? If a company is overleveraged—that is, if it has a heavy debt load compared with its equity—borrowing the money to pay for the system may not be a good idea. Perhaps it will need to issue new stock and therefore increase its equity investment. Making decisions about how to get the capital required to run a business is the job of the chief financial officer and the treasurer, not the IT manager. But an understanding of the company's cash and debt situation should inform the manager's decision about when to buy the new equipment.

Any manager, in short, may want to step back now and then and look at the big picture. Consider not just the one line item on the income statement that you are focusing on, but the balance sheet as well (and the cash flow statement, which we'll get to shortly). When you do, your thinking, your work, and your decisions will be "deeper"—that is, they will consider more factors, and you'll be able to talk about their impact with greater nuance and understanding. Besides, imagine talking to your CFO about the impact of profit on equity: he's likely to be impressed (even shocked).

ASSESSING A COMPANY'S HEALTH

Remember, we said at the beginning of this part that savvy investors typically pore over a company's balance sheet first. The reason is that the balance sheet answers a lot of questions—questions like the following:

- *Is the company solvent?* That is, do its assets outweigh its liabilities, so that owners' equity is a positive number?

- *Can the company pay its bills?* Here the important numbers are current assets, particularly cash, compared with current liabilities. More on this in part 5, on ratios.

- *Has owners' equity been growing over time?* A comparison of balance sheets over a period of time will show whether the company has been moving in the right direction.

These are simple, basic questions, of course. But investors can learn much more from detailed examination of the balance sheet and its footnotes and from comparisons between the balance sheet and other statements. How important is goodwill to the company's "total assets" line? What assumptions have been used to determine depreciation, and how important is that? (Remember Waste Management.) Is the cash line increasing over time—usually a good sign—or is it decreasing? If owners' equity is rising, is that because the company has required an infusion of capital, or is it because the company has been making money?

The balance sheet, in short, helps to show whether a company is financially healthy. All the statements help you make that judgment, but the balance sheet—a company's cumulative GPA—may be the most important of all.

Part Three
Toolbox

EXPENSE? OR CAPITAL EXPENDITURE?

When a company buys a piece of capital equipment, the cost doesn't show up on the income statement; rather, the new asset appears on the balance sheet, and only the depreciation appears on the income statement as a charge against profit. You might think the distinction between *expense* (showing up on the income statement) and *capital expenditure* (showing up on the balance sheet) would be clear and simple. But of course it isn't. Indeed, it's a prime canvas for the art of finance.

Consider that taking a big item off the income statement and putting it on the balance sheet—so that only the depreciation shows up as a charge against profit—can have the effect of increasing profit considerably. WorldCom, mentioned in chapter 1, is the classic case study. A large portion of WorldCom's expenses consisted of so-called line costs. These were fees it paid to local phone companies to use their phone lines. Line costs were normally treated as ordinary operating expenses, but you could argue (albeit incorrectly) that some of them were actually investments in new markets and wouldn't start paying off for years. That was the logic pursued by CFO Scott Sullivan, anyway, who began "capitalizing" his company's line costs. Bingo: these expenses disappeared off the income statement, and profits rose by billions of dollars. To Wall Street, it appeared that WorldCom was suddenly generating much more in profits than it had before—and no one caught on until later, when the whole house of cards collapsed.

WorldCom took an overaggressive approach toward capitalizing its costs and ended up in hot water. But some companies will treat the occasional questionable item as a capital expenditure just to pump up their earnings a little. Does yours?

THE IMPACT OF MARK-TO-MARKET ACCOUNTING

Mark-to-market accounting, as we explained in chapter 11, involves valuing certain financial assets at their current prices rather than by their historical cost. The financial crisis that began in 2008 was in many respects a mark-to-market accounting crisis. Let's see why.

First, consider a simplified accounting of a bank's assets and liabilities. Its assets include loans made to others plus cash. Its liabilities include customer deposits such as checking and savings account balances. Fundamentally, a bank makes money by taking deposits and then lending that money out at a higher rate than it must pay its depositors.

In the 1980s, however, many savings and loan institutions—small banks that specialized in home mortgages—found themselves in a pickle. Their assets consisted mainly of long-term mortgages, which paid a relatively low interest rate. Meanwhile, depositors were demanding high interest rates on their deposits because inflation at the time was so high. To keep the depositors from withdrawing their funds, the S&Ls had to pay out more in interest than they were making on their assets. In a matter of months, hundreds of them became insolvent.

As a result of this issue, the government then began requiring financial institutions to maintain a balance between the duration of their loans and their deposits. That meant the banks couldn't offer long-term mortgages because depositors didn't want to tie up their money for that long. To solve the problem, the government commissioned two enterprises known as Fannie Mae and Freddie Mac to buy mortgages from the banks, package them into securities, and sell the securities to investors. These new instruments were known as mortgage-backed securities, and they were highly popular. They paid a good interest rate, and they seemed safe. The loans that Freddie and Fannie could buy had to meet certain requirements, and were known as prime loans.

After several years, other financial organizations began buying mortgages that did not fit the requirements for prime loans. They packaged these riskier "subprime" loans into securities and sold the securities to investors. Soon, even Freddie and Fannie were allowed to buy subprime mortgages, since the government believed that doing so would help more people become homeowners. All this created an environment where almost anybody could get a mortgage. That boosted demand for housing, which drove up housing prices and seemed to provide investors even more safety. With home prices rising, any default would always be covered by higher home values.

Since banks were originating these mortgages and selling them within a week to a ready market, the mortgages were considered mark-to-market assets on their balance sheets. Many banks held billions of dollars' worth of mortgages that they planned to resell for a profit. But then the housing market began its collapse. Prices fell. More homeowners defaulted. Most investors quit buying the mortgage-backed securities, and the middlemen who created them quit buying mortgages from the banks. With no ready buyers, the value of the mortgages held by the banks plunged.

Now let's go back to the mark-to-market rule, which said that the bank must mark these mortgages down to their current market value. If a bank held $10 billion worth of mortgages and the market dropped 10 percent, it would have to record a loss of $1 billion. That might wipe out all its equity, and the bank would have to be shut down.

In the fourth quarter of 2008, something very much like this scenario happened to hundreds of banks across the United States. News reports told the public about the "toxic" assets the banks couldn't sell. The government responded with the $800 billion Troubled Asset Relief Program (TARP) to bail out many of the troubled banks. In many cases, however, the banks were not actually insolvent: borrowers were still paying, and the banks could rely on the interest rate spread to meet the needs of depositors. But the mark-to-market rule drove them to their knees.

Since the crisis, the Financial Accounting Standards Board has modified the mark-to-market rules for financial institutions in ways that limits the losses a bank might need to take in such circumstances. But the board's moves were too little and too late to affect the crisis.

Part Four

Cash Is King

15

Cash Is a Reality Check

MANY MANAGERS ARE TOO BUSY worrying about income-statement measures such as EBITDA to give cash much notice. Boards of directors and outside analysts sometimes focus too heavily on the balance sheet. But there is one investor who watches cash closely: Warren Buffett.

Warren Buffett may be the single greatest investor of all time. His company, Berkshire Hathaway, has invested in scores of companies and achieved astonishing results. From 2006 through 2010, the book value of Berkshire Hathaway—a conservative indicator of its worth—rose at an average annual rate of 10.0 percent, compared with 2.3 percent for the S&P 500, a broad gauge of publicly traded stocks. That continued an exceptional investment performance dating all the way back to 1965. How does Buffett do it? Many people have written books attempting to explain his investing philosophy and analytical approach. But in our opinion it all boils down to just three simple precepts. First, he evaluates a business on its long-term rather than its short-term prospects. Second, he always looks for businesses he understands. (This led him to avoid many Internet-related investments.) And third, when he examines financial statements, he places the greatest emphasis on a measure of cash flow that he calls *owner earnings*. Warren Buffett has taken financial intelligence to a whole new level, and his net worth reflects it. How interesting that, to him, cash is king.

Owner Earnings

Owner earnings is a measure of the company's ability to generate cash over a period of time. We like to say it is the money an owner could take out of his business and spend for his own benefit. Owner earnings is an important measure because it allows for the continuing capital expenditures that will be necessary to maintain a healthy business. Profit and even operating cash flow measures do not. More about owner earnings in the toolbox at the end of this part.

WHY CASH IS KING

Let's look at that third element of the financial statements—cash—in more detail. Why target cash flow as a key measure of business performance? Why not just profit, as found on the income statement? Why not just a company's assets or owners' equity, as revealed by the balance sheet? For one thing, profit is not the same as cash, as we explain in chapter 16. Profit is based on promises, not money coming in. So if you want to know whether your company has cash to pay employees, pay its bills, and even invest in equipment, you need to study cash flow.

Then, too, the income statement and balance sheet, however useful, have all sorts of potential biases, a result of the assumptions and estimates that are built into them. Cash is different. Look at a company's cash flow statement, and you are indirectly peering into its bank account. Today, after all the financial turmoil of the past fifteen years, cash flow is the darling of Wall Street. It has become a prominent measure by which analysts evaluate companies. But Warren Buffett has been looking at cash all along because he knows that it's the number least affected by the art of finance.

Why do some managers fail to pay attention to cash? There are any number of reasons. In the past, nobody asked them to (though this is beginning to change). Folks in the finance organization often believe that cash is *their* concern and nobody else's. But often, the reason is simply a lack of financial intelligence. Managers don't understand the accounting rules that determine profit, so they assume that profit is pretty much the same as net cash coming in. Some don't believe that their actions affect their company's cash situation; others may believe it, but they don't understand how.

There's another reason, too, which is that the language on the cash flow statement is a little arcane. Most cash flow statements are hard for a nonfinancial person to read, let alone understand. But talk about an investment that pays off: if you take the time to understand cash, you can cut right through a lot of the smoke and mirrors created by your company's financial artists. You can see how good a job your company is doing at turning profit into cash. You can spot early warning signs of trouble, and you will know how to manage so that cash flow is healthy. Cash is a reality check.

One of us, Joe, learned about the importance of cash when he was a financial analyst at a small company early in his career. The company was struggling, and everyone knew it. One day the CFO and the controller were both out golfing and were unreachable. (This was in the days before everybody had a cell phone, which shows you how old Joe is.) The banker called the office and talked with the CEO. Evidently, the CEO didn't like what he was hearing from the banker and felt he had better talk to someone in accounting or finance. So he passed the call to Joe. Joe learned from the banker that the company's credit line was maxed out. "Given that tomorrow is payday," the banker said, "we're curious about what your plan is to cover payroll." Thinking quickly (as always), Joe replied, "Um—can I call you back?" He then did some research and found that a big customer owed the company a good deal of money and that the check—really—was in the mail. He told the banker this, and the banker agreed to cover payroll, provided Joe brought the customer's check to the bank the minute it arrived.

In fact, the check arrived that same day, but after the bank closed. So first thing the next morning, Joe drove to the bank, check in hand. He arrived a few minutes before the bank opened, and noticed that a line had already formed. In fact, he saw that several employees from his company were already there, holding their paychecks. One of them accosted him and said, "So you figured it out too, huh?" "Figured what out?" Joe asked. The guy looked at him with something resembling pity. "Figured *it* out. We've been taking our paychecks to the bank every Friday first break we got. We cash 'em and then deposit the cash in our own banks. That way, we can make sure the checks don't bounce—and if the bank won't cash them, we can spend the rest of the day looking for a job."

That was one day Joe's financial intelligence took a big leap upward. He realized what Warren Buffett already knew: it's cash that keeps a company alive, and cash flow is a critical measure of its financial health. You need people to run the business—any business. You need a place of business, telephones, electricity, computers, supplies, and so on. And you can't pay for all these things with profits, because profits aren't real money. Cash is.

16

Profit ≠ Cash

(and You Need Both)

WHY IS PROFIT NOT THE SAME AS CASH COMING IN? Some reasons are pretty obvious: cash may be coming in from loans or from investors, and that cash isn't going to show up on the income statement at all. But even operating cash flow, which we'll explain in detail in chapter 17, is not at all the same as net profit. There are three essential reasons:

- *Revenue is booked at sale.* One reason is the fundamental fact that we explained in our discussion of the income statement. A sale is recorded whenever a company delivers a product or service. Ace Printing Company delivers $1,000 worth of brochures to a customer; Ace Printing Company records revenues of $1,000, and theoretically it could record a profit by subtracting its costs and expenses from that revenue. But no cash has changed hands, because Ace's customer typically has thirty days or more to pay. Since profit starts with revenue, it always reflects customers' promises to pay. Cash flow, by contrast, always reflects cash transactions.

- *Expenses are matched to revenue.* The purpose of the income statement is to tote up all the costs and expenses associated with generating revenue during a given time period. As we saw in part 2, however, those expenses may not be the ones that were actually paid during that time period. Some may have been paid for earlier (as with the start-up that had to pay for a year's rent in advance). Most will be paid for later, when vendors' bills come due. So the expenses on the income statement do not reflect cash going out. The cash flow statement, however, always measures cash in and out the door during a particular time period.

- *Capital expenditures don't count against profit.* Remember the toolbox at the end of part 3? A capital expenditure doesn't appear on the income statement when it occurs; only as the item depreciates is its cost charged against revenue. So a company can buy trucks, machinery, computer systems, and so on, and the expense will appear on the income statement only gradually, over the useful life of each item. Cash, of course, is another story: all those items often are paid for long before they have been fully depreciated, and the cash used to pay for them will be reflected in the cash flow statement.

You may be thinking that in the long run cash flow will pretty much track net profit. Accounts receivable will be collected, so sales will turn into cash. Accounts payable will be paid, so expenses will more or less even out from one time period to the next. And capital expenditures will be depreciated, so that over time the charges against revenue from depreciation will more or less equal the cash being spent on new assets. All this is true, to a degree, at least for a mature, well-managed company. But the difference between profit and cash can create all sorts of mischief in the meantime.

PROFIT WITHOUT CASH

We'll illustrate this point by comparing two simple companies with two dramatically different profit and cash positions.

Sweet Dreams Bakery is a new cookies-and-cakes manufacturer that supplies specialty grocery stores. The founder has lined up orders based on her unique home-style recipes, and she's ready to launch on January 1. We'll assume she has $10,000 cash in the bank, and we'll also assume that in the first three months her sales are $20,000, $30,000, and $45,000. Cost of goods sold is 60 percent of sales, and her monthly operating expenses are $10,000.

Just by eyeballing those numbers, you can see she'll soon be making a profit. In fact, the simplified income statements for the first three months look like this:

	January	February	March
Sales	$20,000	$30,000	$45,000
COGS	12,000	18,000	27,000
Gross profit	8,000	12,000	18,000
Expenses	10,000	10,000	10,000
Net profit	$(2,000)	$ 2,000	$ 8,000

A simplified cash flow statement, however, would tell a different story. Sweet Dreams Bakery has an agreement with its vendors to pay for the ingredients and other supplies it buys in thirty days. But those specialty groceries that the company sells to? They're kind of precarious, and they take sixty days to pay their bills. So here's what happens to Sweet Dreams's cash situation:

- In *January*, Sweet Dreams collects nothing from its customers. At the end of the month, all it has is $20,000 in receivables from its sales. Luckily, it does not have to pay anything out for the ingredients it uses, since its vendors expect to be paid in thirty days. (We'll assume that the COGS figure is all for ingredients, because the owner herself does all the baking.) But the company does have to pay expenses—rent, utilities, and so on. So *all* of the initial $10,000 in cash goes out the door to pay expenses, and Sweet Dreams is left with no cash in the bank.

- In *February*, Sweet Dreams still hasn't collected anything. (Remember, the customers pay in sixty days). At the end of the month, it has $50,000 in receivables—January's $20,000 plus February's $30,000—but *still* no cash. Meanwhile, Sweet Dreams now has to pay for the ingredients and supplies for January ($12,000), and it has another month's worth of expenses ($10,000). So it's now in the hole by $22,000.

Can the owner turn this around? Surely, in March those rising profits will improve the cash picture! Alas, no.

- In *March*, Sweet Dreams finally collects on its January sales, so it has $20,000 in cash coming in the door, leaving it only $2,000 short against its end-of-February cash position. But now it has to pay for February's COGS of $18,000 plus March's expenses of $10,000. So at the end of March, it ends up $30,000 in the hole—a worse position than at the end of February.

What's going on here? The answer is that Sweet Dreams is growing. Its sales increase every month, meaning that it must pay more each month for its ingredients. Eventually, its operating expenses will increase as well, as the owner has to hire more people. The other problem is the disparity between the fact that Sweet Dreams must pay its vendors in thirty days while waiting sixty days for receipts from its customers. In effect, it has to front the cash for thirty days—*and as long as sales are increasing, it will never be able to catch up unless it finds additional sources of cash.* As fictional and oversimplified as Sweet Dreams may be, this is precisely how profitable companies go out of business. It is one reason why so many small companies fail in their first year. They simply run out of cash.

CASH WITHOUT PROFIT

But now let's look at another sort of profit/cash disparity.

Fine Apparel is another start-up. It sells expensive men's clothing, and it's located in a part of town frequented by businessmen and well-to-do tourists. Its sales for the first three months are $50,000, $75,000, and $95,000—again, a healthy growth trend. Its cost of goods sold is 70 percent of sales, and its monthly operating expenses are $30,000 (high rent!). For the sake of comparison, we'll say it too begins the period with $10,000 in the bank.

So Fine Apparel's income statement for these months looks like this:

	January	February	March
Sales	$ 50,000	$75,000	$95,000
COGS	35,000	52,500	66,500
Gross profit	15,000	22,500	28,500
Expenses	30,000	30,000	30,000
Net profit	$(15,000)	$ (7,500)	$ (1,500)

It hasn't yet turned the corner on profitability, though it is losing less money each month. Meanwhile, what does its cash picture look like? As a retailer, of course, it collects the money on each sale immediately. And we'll assume that Fine Apparel was able to negotiate good terms with its vendors, paying them in sixty days.

- In *January*, it begins with $10,000 and adds $50,000 in cash sales. It doesn't have to pay for any cost of goods sold yet, so the only cash out the door is that $30,000 in expenses. End-of-the-month bank balance: $30,000.
- In *February*, it adds $75,000 in cash sales and still doesn't pay anything for cost of goods sold. So the month's net cash after the $30,000 in expenses is $45,000. Now the bank balance is $75,000!
- In *March*, it adds $95,000 in cash sales, pays for January's supplies ($35,000) and March's expenses ($30,000). Net cash in for the month is $30,000, and the bank balance is now $105,000.

Cash-based businesses—retailers, restaurants, and so on—can thus get an equally skewed picture of their situation. In this case Fine Apparel's bank balance is climbing every month even though the company is unprofitable. That's fine for a while, and it will continue to be fine so long as the company holds down expenses so that it can turn the corner on profitability. But the owner has to be careful: if he's lulled into thinking that his business is doing great and he can increase those expenses, he's liable to continue on the unprofitable path. If he fails to attain profitability, *eventually he will run out of cash.*

Fine Apparel, too, has its real-world parallels. Every cash-based business, from tiny Main Street shops to giants such as Amazon.com and Dell, has the luxury of taking the customer's money before it must pay for its costs and expenses. It enjoys the "float"—and if it is growing, that float will grow ever larger. But ultimately, the company must be profitable by the standards of the income statement; cash flow in the long run is no protection against unprofitability. In the apparel example, the losses on the books will eventually lead to negative cash flow; just as profits eventually lead to cash, losses eventually use up cash. It's the *timing* of those cash flows that we are trying to understand here.

Understanding the difference between profit and cash is a key to increasing your financial intelligence. It is a foundational concept, one that many managers haven't had an opportunity to learn. And it opens a whole new window of opportunity to ask questions and make smart decisions. For example:

- *Finding the right kind of expertise.* The two situations we described in this chapter require different skills. If a company is profitable but short on cash, then it needs financial expertise—someone capable of lining up additional financing. If a company has cash but is unprofitable, it needs operational expertise, meaning someone capable of bringing down costs or generating additional revenue without adding costs. So not only do financial statements tell you what is going on in the company, they also can tell you what kind of expertise you need to hire.
- *Making good decisions about timing.* Informed decisions on *when* to take an action can increase a company's effectiveness. Take Setpoint as an example. When Joe isn't out training people in business literacy, he is CFO of Setpoint, a company that builds factory-automation systems and other products. Managers at the company know that the first quarter of the year, when many orders for automation systems come in, is the most profitable for the business. But cash is always tight because Setpoint must pay out cash to buy components and pay contractors. The next quarter, Setpoint's cash flow typically improves because receivables from the prior quarter are collected, but profits slow down. Setpoint managers have learned that it's better to buy capital equipment for the business in the second quarter rather than the first, even though the second quarter is traditionally less profitable, just because there's more cash available to pay for it.

The ultimate lesson here is that companies need both profit and cash. They are different, and a healthy business requires both.

17

The Language of Cash Flow

YOU'D THINK A CASH FLOW STATEMENT would be easy to read. Since cash is real money, there are no assumptions and estimates incorporated in the numbers. Cash coming in is a positive number, cash going out is a negative one, and net cash is simply the sum of the two. In fact, though, we find that most nonfinancial managers (and even some financial folks, as we've learned in working with many finance departments) take a while to understand a cash flow statement. One reason is that the labels on the statement's categories can be confusing. A second reason is that the positives and the negatives aren't always clear. (A typical line item might say, "(increase)/decrease in accounts receivable," followed by a positive or a negative number. Is it an increase or a decrease?) A final reason is that it can be tough to see the relationship between the cash flow statement and the other two financial statements.

We'll take up the last issue in chapter 18. Right now, let's just sit down with a cash flow statement and learn the basic vocabulary.

TYPES OF CASH FLOW

The statement shows the cash moving into a business, called the *inflows*, and the cash moving out of a business, called the *outflows*. These are divided into three main categories.

Cash From or Used in Operating Activities

At times you'll see slight variations to this language, such as "cash provided by or used for operating activities." Whatever the exact language, this category includes all the cash flow, in and out, that is related to the actual operations of the business. It includes the cash customers send in when they pay their bills. It includes the cash the company pays out in salaries, to vendors, and to the landlord, along with all the other cash it must spend to keep the doors open and the business operating.

Cash From or Used in Investing Activities

This is one of the labels that can be confusing. *Investing activities* in this context refers to investments made by the company, not by its owners. A key subcategory here is cash spent on capital investments—that is, the purchase of assets. If the company buys a truck or a machine, the cash it pays out shows up on this part of the statement. Conversely, if the company sells a truck or a machine (or any other asset), the cash it receives shows up here. This section also includes investment in acquisitions or financial securities—anything, in short, that involves the buying or selling of company assets.

Cash From or Used in Financing Activities

Financing refers to borrowing and paying back loans on the one hand, and transactions between a company and its shareholders on the other. So if a company receives a loan, the proceeds show up in this category. If a company gets an equity investment from a shareholder, that, too, shows up here. Should the company pay off the principal on a loan, buy back its own

Financing a Company

How a company is financed refers to how it gets the cash it needs to start up or expand. Ordinarily, a company is financed through debt, equity, or both. *Debt* means borrowing money from banks, family members, or other creditors. *Equity* means getting people to buy stock in the company.

stock, or pay a dividend to its shareholders, those expenditures of cash also would appear in this category. Here again is some label confusion: if a shareholder invests more money in a company, the cash involved shows up under financing, not investing.

WHAT EACH CATEGORY TELLS YOU

You can see right away that there is a lot of useful information in the cash flow statement. The first category shows operating cash flow, which in many ways is the single most important number indicating the health of a business. A company with a consistently healthy operating cash flow is *probably* profitable, and it is probably doing a good job of turning its profits into cash. A healthy operating cash flow, moreover, means that it can finance more of its growth internally, without either borrowing or selling more stock.

The second category shows how much cash the company is spending on investments in its future. If the number is low relative to the size of the company, it may not be investing much at all; management may be treating the business as a "cash cow," milking it for the cash it can generate while not investing in future growth. If the number is high relative to company size, it may suggest that management has high hopes for the future of the company. Of course, what counts as high or low will depend on the type of company it is. A service company, for instance, typically invests less in assets than a manufacturing company. So your analysis has to reflect the big picture of the company you're assessing.

The third category shows to what extent the company is dependent on outside financing. Look at this category over time, and you can see whether

Buying Back Stock

If a company has extra cash and believes that its stock is trading at a price that is lower than it ought to be, it may buy back some of its shares. The effect is to decrease the number of shares outstanding and hence to increase the possibility that the price will rise.

the company is a net borrower (borrowing more than it is paying off). You can also see whether it has been selling new shares to outside investors or buying back its own stock.

Finally, the cash flow statement allows you to calculate Warren Buffett's famous owner earnings metric, known on Wall Street as *free cash flow*. (See the toolbox at the end of this part.)

Wall Street in recent years has been focusing more and more on the cash flow statement. For example, many analysts have begun comparing parts of the income statement to parts of the cash flow statement to ensure that the company is converting its profit into cash. Also, as Buffett knows, there is much less room for manipulation of the numbers on the cash flow statement than on the others. To be sure, "less room" doesn't mean "no room." For example, if a company is trying to show good cash flow in a particular quarter, it may delay paying vendors or employee bonuses until the next quarter. Unless a company delays payments over and over, however—and eventually, vendors who don't get paid will stop providing goods and services—the effects are significant only in the short term.

18

How Cash Connects with Everything Else

ONCE YOU'VE LEARNED TO READ THE CASH FLOW STATEMENT, you can simply take it the way it comes and inspect it for what it tells you about your company's cash situation. Then you can figure out how you affect it—how you as a manager can help better the business's cash position. We'll spell out some of these opportunities in chapter 19.

But if you're the type of person who enjoys a puzzle—who likes to understand the logic of what you're looking at—then stick with us through this chapter. Because it may have already dawned on you: *you can calculate a cash flow statement just by looking at the income statement and two balance sheets.*

The calculations aren't hard: they involve no more than adding and subtracting. But it's easy to get lost in the process. The reason is that accountants don't just have a special language and a special set of tools and techniques; they also have a certain way of thinking. They understand that profit as reported on the income statement is the result of certain rules, assumptions, estimates, and calculations. They understand that assets as reported on the balance sheet aren't "really" worth what the balance sheet says, again because of the rules, assumptions, and estimates that go into valuing them. But accountants also understand that the art of finance, as we have called it, doesn't exist in the abstract. Ultimately, all those rules, assumptions, and estimates have to provide us with useful information about the real world. And since in finance the real world is represented by cash, the balance sheet and the income statement must have some logical relationship to the cash flow statement.

You can see the connections in common transactions. For example, take a credit sale of $100. It shows up as:

- an increase of $100 in accounts receivable on the balance sheet, and
- an increase in sales of $100 on the income statement

When the customer pays the bill, here's what happens:

- accounts receivable decreases by $100, and
- cash increases by $100

These changes both appear on the balance sheet. But because cash is now involved, the transaction affects the cash flow statement as well.

You can watch the effect of all sorts of transactions in just this manner. Say a company buys $100 worth of inventory. The balance sheet records two changes: accounts payable rises by $100 and inventory rises by $100. When the company pays the bill, accounts payable decreases by $100 and cash decreases by $100—again, both on the balance sheet. When that inventory is sold (either intact, as by a retailer, or incorporated into a product by a manufacturer), $100 worth of cost of goods sold will be recorded on the income statement. The cash parts of these transactions—the original disbursement of cash to cover the $100 in accounts payable and the later receipt of cash from the sale of finished goods—will show up on the cash flow statement.

So all these transactions ultimately have an effect on the income statement, the balance sheet, and the cash flow statement. In fact, most transactions eventually find their way onto all three. To show you more of the specific connections, let us walk you through how accountants use the income statement and two balance sheets to calculate cash flow.

RECONCILING PROFIT AND CASH

The first exercise in this process is to reconcile *profit* to *cash*. The question you're trying to answer here is pretty simple: given that we have $X in net profit, what effect does that have on our cash flow?

We start with net profit for this reason: if every transaction were completely in cash, and if there were no noncash expenses such as depreciation, then net profit and operating cash flow would be identical. But since in most businesses everything isn't a cash transaction, we need to determine which line items on the income statement and the balance sheet had the effect of increasing or decreasing cash—in other words, making operating cash flow *different* from net profit. As accountants put it, we need to find "adjustments" to net profit that, when they are added up, let us arrive at the changes in cash flow.

One such adjustment is in accounts receivable. In any given time period, a company takes in some cash from receivables. That decreases the A/R line on the balance sheet. However, the company is also making more credit sales, which adds to the A/R line. We can "net out" the cash figure from these two kinds of transactions by looking at the *change* in receivables from one balance sheet to the next. (Remember, the balance sheet is for a specific day, so changes can be seen when you compare two balance sheets.)

Imagine, for example, that your company has $100 in receivables on the balance sheet at the start of the month. You take in $75 in cash during the month, and you make $100 worth of new credit sales. Here's how you calculate the A/R line at the end of the month:

$$\$100 - \$75 + \$100 = \$125$$

Reconciliation

In a financial context, reconciliation means getting the cash line on a company's balance sheet to match the actual cash the company has in the bank—sort of like balancing your checkbook, but on a larger scale.

Since you began the month with $100 in receivables, the change in receivables from the beginning of the period to the end is $25. Note that the change is also equal to new sales ($100) minus cash received ($75). To put it differently, cash received is equal to new sales minus the change in receivables.

Another adjustment is depreciation. Depreciation is deducted from operating profit on the way to calculating net profit. But depreciation is a noncash expense, as we have learned; it has no effect on cash flow. So you have to add it back in.

A START-UP COMPANY

Clear? Probably not. So let's imagine a very simple start-up company, with sales of $100 in the first month. The cost of goods sold during the month is $50, other expenses are $15, and depreciation is $10. You know that the income statement for the month will look like this:

Income Statement	
Sales	$100
COGS	50
Gross profit	50
Expenses	15
Depreciation	10
Net profit	$ 25

Let's assume that the sales are all receivables—no cash has yet come in—and COGS is all in payables. Using this information, we can construct two partial balance sheets:

Assets	Beginning of Month	End of Month	Change
Accounts receivable	0	$100	$100
Liabilities			
Accounts payable	0	$ 50	$ 50

Now we can take the first step in constructing a cash flow statement. The key rule here is that if an asset *increases,* cash *decreases*—so we *subtract* the increase from net profit. With a liability, the opposite is true. If liabilities *increase,* cash *increases* too—so we *add* the increase to net income.

Here are the calculations:

Start with net profit	$ 25
Subtract increase in A/R	(100)
Add increase in A/P	50
Add in depreciation	10
Equals: net change in cash	$ (15)

You can see that this is true, because the only cash expense the company had during the period was $15 in expenses. With a real company, however, you can't confirm your results just by eyeballing them, so you need to calculate the cash flow statement scrupulously according to the same rules.

A REALISTIC COMPANY

Let's try it with a more complex example. Here (for easy reference) are the income statement and balance sheets for the imaginary company whose financials appear in the appendix:

Income Statement
(in millions)

	Year ending December 31, 2012
Sales	$8,689
Cost of goods sold	6,756
Gross profit	**$1,933**
Sales, general, and administrative (SG&A)	$1,061
Depreciation	239
Other income	19
EBIT	**$ 652**
Interest expense	191
Taxes	213
Net profit	**$ 248**

Balance Sheets
(in millions)

	12/31/2012	12/31/2011
Assets		
Cash and cash equivalents	$ 83	$ 72
Accounts receivable	1,312	1,204
Inventory	1,270	1,514
Other current assets and accruals	85	67
Total current assets	2,750	2,857
Property, plant, and equipment	2,230	2,264
Other long-term assets	213	233
Total assets	**$5,193**	**$5,354**
Liabilities		
Accounts payable	$1,022	$1,129
Credit line	100	150
Current portion of long-term debt	52	51
Total current liabilities	1,174	1,330
Long-term debt	1,037	1,158
Other long-term liabilities	525	491
Total liabilities	**$2,736**	**$2,979**
Shareholders' equity		
Common stock, $1 par value (100,000,000 authorized, 74,000,000 outstanding in 2012 and 2011)	$ 74	$ 74
Additional paid-in capital	1,110	1,110
Retained earnings	1,273	1,191
Total shareholders' equity	**$2,457**	**$2,375**
Total liabilities and shareholders' equity	**$5,193**	**$5,354**

2012 Footnotes:

Depreciation	*$239*
Number of common shares (millions)	*74*
Earnings per share	*$3.35*
Dividend per share	*$2.24*

The same logic applies as in the simple example we gave earlier:

- Look at every change from one balance sheet to the next.
- Determine whether the change resulted in an increase or a decrease in cash.
- Then add or subtract the amount to or from net income.

Here are the steps:

Observation	Action
Start with net profit, $248	———
Depreciation was $239	Add that noncash expense to net profit
Accounts receivable increased by $108	An asset increases. So subtract that increase from net profit
Inventory declined by $244	An asset decreases. So add that decrease to net profit
Other current assets rose by $18	Subtract that increase from net profit
PPE rose by $205 (after adjusting for depreciation of $239—see note 1)	Subtract that increase from net profit
Other long-term assets decreased by $20	Add that decrease to net profit
Accounts payable decreased by $107	A liability decreases. So subtract that decrease from net profit
Credit line decreased by $50	Subtract that decrease from net profit
Current portion of long-term debt rose by $1	A liability increases. So add that increase to net profit
Long-term debt decreased by $121	Subtract that decrease from net profit
Other long-term liabilities increased by $34	Add that increase to net profit
Shareholders equity increased by $82	(See note 2)

Note 1: Why do we need to adjust for depreciation when looking at the change in property, plant, and equipment (PPE)? Remember that every year PPE on the balance sheet is lowered by the amount of depreciation charged to the assets in the account. So if you had a fleet of trucks that were acquired for $100,000, the balance sheet immediately after the acquisition would include $100,000 for trucks on the PPE line. If depreciation on the trucks was $10,000 for the year, then at the end of twelve months, the line in PPE for trucks would be $90,000. But depreciation is a noncash expense, and since we're trying to arrive at a cash number, we have to "factor out" depreciation by adding it back in.

Note 2: Notice the dividends footnoted on the balance sheet? Multiply the dividend times the number of shares outstanding and you get roughly $166 million (which we're representing as just $166). Net income of $248 minus the dividend of $166 equals $82—the precise amount by which shareholders equity increased. This is the amount of profit that stayed in the company as retained earnings. If there is no dividend paid out or new stock sold, then the cash provided or used by equity financing would be zero. Equity would simply increase or decrease by the amount of profit or loss in the period.

Now we can construct a cash flow statement along the following lines. Of course, with a full balance sheet like this one, you have to put the change in cash in the right categories as well. The words on the right show where each number comes from:

Cash Flow Statement
(in millions)

Year ended December 31, 2012		
Cash from operating activities		
Net profit	$248	net profit on income statement
Depreciation	239	depreciation from income statement
Accounts receivable	(108)	change in A/R from 2011 to 2012
Inventory	244	change in inventory
Other current assets	(18)	change in other current assets
Accounts payable	(107)	change in A/P
Cash from operations	**$498**	

Cash from investing activities		
Property, plant, and equipment	$(205)	PPE change adjusted for depreciation
Other long-term assets	20	change from balance sheet
Cash from investing	**$(185)**	
Cash from financing activities		
Credit line	$ (50)	change in short-term credit
Current portion of long-term debt	1	change in current long-term debt
Long-term debt	(121)	change from balance sheet
Other long-term liabilities	34	change from balance sheet
Equity	(166)	dividends paid
Cash from financing	**$(302)**	
Change in cash	11	add the three sections together
Cash at beginning	72	from 2011 balance sheet
Cash at end	**$ 83**	change in cash + beginning cash

The "cash at end," of course, equals the cash balance on the ending balance sheet.

This is a complicated exercise! But you can see that there's a good deal of beauty and subtlety in all the connections (maybe only if you are an accountant). Go beneath the surface a little—or, to use another metaphor, read between the lines—and you can see how all the numbers relate to one another. Your financial intelligence is on the way up, as is your appreciation of the art of finance.

19

Why Cash Matters

OF COURSE, by now you may be saying to yourself, "So what? All this is cumbersome to figure out, and why do I care?"

For starters, let's see what our sample company's cash flow statement reveals. In terms of operations, it is certainly doing a good job of generating cash. Operating cash flow is considerably higher than net income. Inventory declined, so it's reasonable to suppose that the company is tightening up its operations. All of this makes for a stronger cash position.

We can also see, however, that there is not a lot of new investment going on. Depreciation outweighed new investment, which makes us wonder if management believes that the company has much of a future. Meanwhile, the company is paying its shareholders a healthy dividend, which may suggest that they value it more for its cash-generating potential than for its future. (Many growing companies don't pay large dividends because they retain the earnings to invest in the business. Some pay no dividends at all.)

Of course, these are all suppositions about our sample company. To really know the truth, you'd have to know a lot more about the company, what business it's in, and so on—the big-picture part of financial intelligence. But if you did know all those things, the cash flow statement would be extraordinarily revealing.

That brings us to your own situation as a manager and to your own company's cash flow. We think there are three big reasons for looking at and trying to understand the cash flow statement.

THE POWER OF UNDERSTANDING CASH FLOW

First, knowing your company's cash situation will help you understand what is going on now, where the business is headed, and what senior management's priorities are likely to be. You need to know not just whether the overall cash position is healthy but specifically where the cash is coming from. Is it from operations? That's a good thing—it means the business is generating cash. Is investing cash flow a sizable negative number? If it isn't, it may mean that the company isn't investing in its future. And what about financing cash flow? If investment money is coming in, that may be an optimistic sign for the future, or it may mean that the company is desperately selling stock to stay afloat. Looking at the cash flow statement may generate a lot of questions, but they are the right ones to be asking. Are we paying off loans? Why or why not? Are we buying equipment? The answers to those questions will reveal a lot about senior management's plans for the company.

Second, you *affect* cash. As we've said before, managers should be focusing on both profit and cash. Of course, their impact is usually limited to operating cash flow—but that's one of the most important measures there is. For instance:

- *Accounts receivable.* If you're in sales, are you selling to customers who pay their bills on time? Do you have a close enough relationship with your customers to talk with them about payment terms? If you're in customer service, do you offer customers the kind of service that will encourage them to pay their bills on time? Is the product free of defects? Are the invoices accurate? Does the mailroom send invoices on a timely basis? Is the receptionist helpful? All these factors help determine how customers feel about your company and indirectly influence how fast they are likely to pay their bills. Disgruntled customers are not known for prompt payments—they like to wait until any dispute is resolved.

- *Inventory.* If you're in engineering, do you request special products all the time? If you do, you may be creating an inventory nightmare. If you're in operations and you like to have lots in stock, just in case, you may be creating a situation in which cash is just sitting on the shelves, when it could be used for something else. Manufacturing and warehouse managers can often reduce inventory hugely by studying and applying the principles of lean enterprise, pioneered at Toyota.

- *Expenses.* Do you defer expenses when you can? Do you consider the timing of cash flow when making purchases? Obviously, we're not saying it's always wise to defer expenses; it's just wise to understand what the cash impact will be when you do decide to spend money, and to take that into account.

- *Giving credit.* Do you give credit to potential customers too easily? Alternatively, do you withhold credit when you should give it? Both decisions affect the company's cash flow and sales, which is why the credit department always has to strike a careful balance.

The list goes on. Maybe you're a plant manager, and you are always recommending buying more equipment, just in case the orders come in. Perhaps you're in IT, and you feel that the company always needs the latest upgrades to its computer systems. All these decisions affect cash flow, and senior management usually understands that very well. If you want to make an effective request, you need to familiarize yourself with the numbers that they're looking at.

Third, managers who understand cash flow tend to be given more responsibilities, and thus tend to advance more quickly, than those who focus purely on the income statement. In the following part, for instance, you'll learn to calculate ratios such as days sales outstanding (DSO), which is a key measure of the company's efficiency in collecting receivables. The faster receivables are collected, the better a company's cash position. You could go to someone in finance and say, "By the way, I notice our DSO has been heading in the wrong direction over the last few months—how can I help turn that around?" Alternatively, you might learn the precepts of lean enterprise, which focus on (among other things) keeping inventories to a minimum. A manager who leads a company in converting to lean thereby frees up huge quantities of cash.

But our general point here is that cash flow is a key indicator of a company's financial health, along with profitability and shareholders' equity.

It's the final link in the triad, and you need all three to assess a company's financial health. It's also the final link in the first level of financial intelligence. You now have a good understanding of all three financial statements. Now it's time to move on to the next level—to put that information to work.

Part Four
Toolbox

FREE CASH FLOW

Several years ago, Wall Street's favorite measure was EBITDA, or earnings before interest, taxes, depreciation, and amortization. Banks loved EBITDA because they believed it was a good indication of future cash flow. But then came a double whammy. During the dot-com boom of the late 1990s, companies such as WorldCom turned out to have cooked their books. So their EBITDA figures were not reliable. When the financial crisis hit in 2008, investors and lenders grew even more wary of any metric tied to the income statement. They realized that income statements are loaded with estimates and assumptions, and that profit shown on these statements is not necessarily real.

So now there's a hot new metric on Wall Street: free cash flow. Some companies have looked at free cash flow for years. Warren Buffett's Berkshire Hathaway is the best-known example, though Buffett calls it *owner earnings.*

You can calculate free cash flow in a couple of different ways, but the most common approach is simple subtraction:

Free cash flow = operating cash flow less net capital expenditures

These figures come directly from the cash flow statement. Operating cash flow (or "cash provided by operating activities") is the total from the top section of the statement. Net capital expenditures are purchases of property, plant, and equipment—a line item in the investing section of the cash flow statement. We use the term *net* capital expenditures because many businesses add back any proceeds from sales of capital equipment (another line in the investing section). Note that net capital expenditures is almost always a negative number, which may create some confusion. Ignore the minus sign! Just subtract the absolute value of that line from operating cash flow. Using our sample financial statements in the appendix, for example, free cash flow for this company would be $498 (cash from operations) less $205 (the amount invested in property, plant, and equipment), or $293 million.

Investors have gravitated to this metric because cash is not subject to estimates and assumptions. It's easy to audit cash balances. Unless the company is simply lying—and this kind of lie is very likely to come out quickly—it really has the cash flow indicated on its statement. Also, whenever capital markets are constrained (as they have often been since 2008), the businesses most able to invest in growth will be those that can generate their own cash.

From a company's point of view, a healthy free cash flow gives it some good options. It can expand operations, make acquisitions, pay off debt, buy back its stock, or pay dividends to shareholders. Companies with weak free cash flow have to get outside financing to do any of that. And, of course, the more free cash flow you have, the more favorably Wall Street will view your stock.

EVEN THE BIG GUYS CAN RUN OUT OF CASH

While teaching a finance module to executives of a *Fortune* 100 company, we were discussing the importance of cash. An attendee raised her hand to recount a story.

It was the first quarter of 2009, she said, and the capital markets were in trouble. One of her clients called. The client had a $100 million credit line with the company's financial division and wanted to draw down the entire amount. She remonstrated, arguing that the client seemed to have plenty of cash on its balance sheet. But the client persisted.

So the executive contacted her company's treasury department and requested that the funds be wired to her client's account. The request was normally a routine exercise for such a large company, but this time the treasury told her that the corporation did not have enough cash to make the transfer. The executive was in shock. "Did I hear you right?" she asked.

And then she said, "Do you really want me to tell the client that our corporation does not have the cash to meet this committed credit line?" Finally, the treasury representative asked her to contact the CEO's office for approval and said he and his colleagues would try to find the cash. Which they eventually did.

How can a big corporation even come close to running out of cash? In fact, the trouble lay behind the scenes. For a week or two in early 2009, the commercial paper window on Wall Street shut down because of all the uncertainty in financial circles. Commercial paper consists of short-term notes or loans to large, stable corporations that typically come due in thirty, sixty, or ninety days. Many large corporations roll over billions of dollars of these low-interest notes to handle their short-term financial needs. This particular company was using many billions of dollars' worth of commercial paper for that purpose. Every week, several billion in notes would come due, and the company would roll this over into new notes. When the market shut down, the corporation was billions of dollars short and had to scramble to find a way to cover the shortfall.

Part Five

Ratios: Learning What the Numbers Are Really Telling You

20

The Power of Ratios

THE EYES MAY OR MAY NOT BE A WINDOW INTO THE SOUL, as Immanuel Kant suggested, but ratios are definitely a window into a company's financial statements. They offer a quick shortcut to understanding what the financials are saying.

There's a classic story that illustrates this point very well. The year was 1997. The notorious "Chainsaw Al" Dunlap had recently become chief executive of Sunbeam, then an independent appliance maker. By the time he arrived at Sunbeam, Dunlap already had a great reputation on Wall Street and a standard *modus operandi*. He would show up at a troubled company, fire the management team, bring in his own people, and immediately start slashing expenses by closing down or selling factories and laying off thousands of employees. Soon the company would be showing a profit because of all those cuts, even though it might not be well positioned for the longer term. Dunlap would then arrange for it to be sold, usually at a premium—which meant that he was often hailed as a champion of shareholder value. Sunbeam's stock jumped more than 50 percent on the news that he'd been hired as CEO.

At Sunbeam, everything went according to the usual plan until Dunlap began readying the company for sale. By then, he had cut the workforce in half, from twelve thousand to six thousand, and was reporting strong profits. Wall Street was so impressed that Sunbeam's stock price had gone through the roof—which, as we noted earlier, turned out to be a major problem. When the investment bankers went out to sell the company, the price was so high that they had trouble identifying prospective buyers. Dunlap's only hope was to boost sales and earnings to a level that could justify the kind of premium a buyer would have to offer for Sunbeam's stock.

ACCOUNTING TRICKS

We now know that Dunlap and his CFO, Russ Kersh, used a whole bag of accounting tricks in that fourth quarter to make Sunbeam look far stronger and more profitable than it actually was. One of the tricks was a perversion of a technique called *bill-and-hold*.

Bill-and-hold is essentially a way of accommodating retailers who want to buy large quantities of products for sale in the future, but put off paying for them until the products are actually being sold. Say that you have a chain of toy stores, and you want to ensure that you have an adequate supply of Barbie dolls for the Christmas season. Sometime in the spring, you might go to Mattel and propose a deal whereby you'll buy a certain number of Barbies, take delivery of them, and even allow Mattel to bill you for them—but you won't pay for the dolls until the Christmas season rolls around and you start selling them. Meanwhile, you'll keep them in a warehouse. It's a good deal for you, since you can count on having the Barbies when you need them, yet you can hold off paying for them until you have decent cash flow. It's also a good deal for Mattel, which can make the sale and record it immediately, even though it has to wait a few more months to collect the cash.

Dunlap figured that a variation on bill-and-hold was one answer to his problem. The fourth quarter was not a particularly strong period for Sunbeam, which made a lot of products geared toward summer—gas grills, for example. So Sunbeam went to major retailers such as Walmart and Kmart and offered to guarantee that they'd have all the grills they wanted for the following summer provided they did their buying in the middle of winter. They'd be billed immediately, but they wouldn't have to pay until spring, when they actually put the goods in the stores. The retailers were cool to the idea. They didn't have anywhere to keep all that stuff, nor did they want to bear the cost of storing the inventory through the winter. "No problem," said Sunbeam. "We'll take care of that for you. We'll lease space near your facilities and cover all the storage costs ourselves."

Supposedly, the retailers agreed to those terms, although an audit conducted after Dunlap was fired failed to turn up a complete paper trail. In any case, Sunbeam went ahead and reported an additional $36 million in sales for the fourth quarter based on the bill-and-hold deals it had initiated. The scam worked well enough to fool most analysts, investors, and even Sunbeam's board of directors, which in early 1998 rewarded Dunlap and other members of the executive team with lucrative new employment contracts. Although they had been on the job for less than a year, they received some $38 million in stock grants, based largely on the mistaken belief that the company had just had a stellar fourth quarter.

But Andrew Shore, a consumer-products analyst with the investment firm Paine Webber, had been following Sunbeam since Dunlap arrived, and now was scrutinizing its financials. He noticed some oddities, like higher-than-normal sales in the fourth quarter. Then he calculated a ratio called *days sales outstanding* (DSO) and found that it was huge, far above what it ought to have been. In effect, it indicated that the company's accounts receivable had gone through the roof. That was a bad sign, so he called a Sunbeam accountant to ask what was going on. The accountant told Shore about the bill-and-hold strategy. Shore realized that Sunbeam, in effect, had already recorded a hefty chunk of sales that would normally appear in the first and second quarters. After discovering this bill-and-hold game and other questionable practices, he promptly downgraded the stock.

The rest, as they say, is history. Dunlap tried to hang on, but the stock plummeted and investors grew wary of what Sunbeam's financials were telling them. Eventually, Dunlap was forced out and Sunbeam went bankrupt—and it all started because Andrew Shore knew enough to dig beneath the surface and find out what was really going on. Ratios such as DSO were a useful tool for Shore, as they can be for you.

ANALYZING RATIOS

Ratios indicate the relationship of one number to another. People use them every day. A baseball player's batting average of .333 shows the relationship between hits and official at bats—one hit for every three at bats. The odds of winning a lottery jackpot, say one in 6 million, show the relationship between winning tickets sold (1) and total tickets sold (6 million). Ratios don't require any complex calculations. To figure a ratio, usually, you just divide one number by another and then express the result as a decimal or as a percentage.

All kinds of people use all kinds of financial ratios in assessing a business. For example:

- Bankers and other lenders examine ratios such as debt-to-equity, which gives them an idea of whether a company will be able to pay back a loan.
- Senior managers watch ratios such as gross margin, which helps them be aware of rising costs or inappropriate discounting.
- Credit managers assess potential customers' financial health by inspecting the quick ratio, which gives them an indication of the customer's supply of ready cash compared with its current liabilities.
- Potential and current shareholders look at ratios such as price-to-earnings, which helps them decide whether a company is valued high or low by comparison with other stocks (and with its own value in previous years).

In this part of the book we'll show you how to calculate many such ratios. The ability to calculate them—to read between the lines of the financials, so to speak—is a mark of financial intelligence. Learning about ratios will give you a host of intelligent questions to ask your boss or CFO. And, of course, we'll show you how to use them to boost your company's performance.

The power of ratios lies in the fact that the numbers in the financial statements by themselves don't reveal the whole story. Is net profit of $10 million a healthy bottom line for a company? Who knows? It depends on the size of the company, on what net profit was last year, on how much net profit was expected to be this year, and on many other variables. If you ask whether a $10 million profit is good or bad, the only possible answer is the one given by the woman in the old joke. Asked how her husband was, she replied, "Compared to what?"

Ratios offer points of comparison and thus tell you more than the raw numbers alone. Profit, for example, can be compared with sales, or with total assets, or with the amount of equity shareholders have invested in the company. A different ratio expresses each relationship, and each gives you a way of gauging whether a $10 million profit is good news or bad news. As we'll see, many of the different line items on the financials are incorporated into ratios. Those ratios help you understand whether the numbers you're looking at are favorable or unfavorable.

What's more, the ratios themselves can be compared. For instance:

- *You can compare ratios with themselves over time.* Is profit relative to sales up or down this year? This level of analysis can reveal some powerful trend lines—and some big warning flags if the ratios are headed in the wrong direction.

- *You can also compare ratios with what was projected.* To pick just one of the ratios we'll be examining in this part, if your inventory turnover is worse than you expected it to be, you need to find out why.

- *You can compare ratios with industry averages.* If you find that your company's key ratios are worse than those of your competitors, you definitely want to figure out the reason. To be sure, not all the ratio results we discuss will be similar from one company to another, even in the same industry. For most, there's a reasonable range. It's when the ratios get outside of that range, as Sunbeam's DSO did, that it's worth your attention.

There are four categories of ratios that managers and other stakeholders in a business typically use to analyze the company's performance: profitability, leverage, liquidity, and efficiency. We will give you examples in each category. Note, however, that many of these formulas can be tinkered with by the financial folks to address specific approaches or concerns. We see this on a regular basis with our clients. The formulas used by one client in Silicon Valley, for example, were highly specific to its business; as a result, it was difficult to compare the company's results to those of a competitor, which also had its own unique formulas. Tinkering of this sort doesn't mean that people are cooking the books, only that they are using their expertise to obtain the most useful information for particular situations (yes, there is art even in formulas). What we will provide are the foundational formulas, the ones you need to learn first. Each provides a different view—like looking into a house through windows on all four sides.

A WORD OF CAUTION

We do want to add a note of caution before we begin. In our experience, some companies focus attention on one or two ratios while ignoring other key ratios and the big picture of the business. For example, every public company concerns itself with earnings per share, which is a ratio that investors watch closely. And many watch net profit margin to the exclusion of ratios that might indicate suboptimal performance in other areas.

When Joe worked at Ford in the early 1990s, for example, he was given the assignment of pricing a certain category of aftermarket parts. Ford wanted a predetermined profit margin on the entire line of parts and required that prices be set accordingly. In Joe's product line, it turned out that Ford had a warehouse full of old Mustang parts that just wouldn't sell. Because Ford's prices were high, would-be buyers could get the parts much cheaper from a junkyard or third-party sellers.

Joe realized that these parts were costing Ford warehousing space, and that they sat on the company's balance sheet as inventory, which as we know ties up cash. But when he suggested deeply discounting the parts to free up space and get them out of inventory, management's answer was simple: no. If we did that, they said, the product line would not hit its profit margin target. So the price discount was never considered.

In our view, Ford at the time was too focused on one ratio, profit margin, while ignoring ratios that might have indicated the value of selling the parts. If it discounted the parts, the margin it received would have been below its target. But overall total profit would have been higher because the parts hadn't been selling at all up to then. Moreover, the company would have freed up warehouse space and converted some of its inventory to cash. Return on assets, free cash flow, and asset turnover, to name a few other ratios, would have improved.

One more caution: when you are looking at ratios, you also need to consider the overall value of the numbers. If Walmart consistently earns a 3 percent profit margin on annual sales of over $400 billion, that is a lot more money than a 30 percent profit margin on a business with $50 million in sales. While ratios are an important piece of the financial puzzle, you always need to put them in context to get the complete picture.

21

Profitability Ratios

The Higher the Better (Mostly)

PROFITABILITY RATIOS help you evaluate a company's ability to generate profits. There are dozens of them, a fact that helps keep the financial folks busy. But here we're going to focus on just the most important. These are really the only ones most managers need to understand and use. Profitability ratios are the most common of ratios. If you get these, you'll be off to a good start in financial statement analysis.

Before we dive in, however, do remember the artful aspects of what we're looking at. Profitability is a measure of a company's ability to generate sales and to control its expenses. None of these numbers is wholly objective. Sales are subject to rules as to when the revenue can be recorded. Expenses are often a matter of estimation, not to say guesswork. Assumptions are built into both sets of numbers. So profit as reported on the income statement is a product of the art of finance, and any ratio based on those numbers will itself reflect all those estimates and assumptions. We don't propose throwing out the baby with the bathwater—the ratios are still useful—only that you keep in mind that estimates and assumptions can always change.

Now, on to the profitability ratios that we promised you.

GROSS PROFIT MARGIN PERCENTAGE

Gross profit, you'll recall, is revenue minus cost of goods sold. *Gross profit margin percentage*, often called gross margin, is simply gross profit divided by revenue, with the result expressed as a percentage. Look at the sample income statement in the appendix, which we'll use to calculate examples of all these ratios. In this case the calculation is as follows:

$$\text{gross margin} = \frac{\text{gross profit}}{\text{revenue}} = \frac{\$1{,}933}{\$8{,}689} = 22.2\%$$

Gross margin shows the basic profitability of the product or service itself, before expenses or overhead are added in. It tells you how much of every sales dollar you get to use in the business—22.2 cents in this example—and (indirectly) how much you must pay out in direct costs (COGS or COS), just to get the product produced or the service delivered. (COGS or COS is 77.8 cents per sales dollar in this example.) It's thus a key measure of a company's financial health. After all, if you can't deliver your products or services at a price that is sufficiently above cost to support the rest of your company, you don't have a chance of earning a net profit.

Trend lines in gross margin are equally important, because they indicate potential problems. Say a company announces great sales numbers in one quarter—better than expected—but then its stock drops. How could that be? Perhaps analysts noted that gross margin percentage was heading downward and assumed that the company must have been doing considerable discounting to record the sales it did. In general, a negative trend in gross margin indicates one of two things (sometimes both). Either the company is under severe price pressure and salespeople are being forced to discount, or else materials and labor costs are rising, driving up COGS or COS. Gross margin thus can be a kind of early-warning light, indicating favorable or unfavorable trends in the marketplace.

OPERATING PROFIT MARGIN PERCENTAGE

Operating profit margin percentage, or operating margin, is a more comprehensive measure of a company's ability to generate profit. Operating profit or EBIT, remember, is gross profit minus operating expenses, so the level of operating profit indicates how well a company is running its entire business from an operational standpoint. Operating margin is just operating profit divided by revenue, with the result expressed as a percentage:

$$\text{operating margin} = \frac{\text{operating profit (EBIT)}}{\text{revenue}} = \frac{\$652}{\$8{,}689} = 7.5\%$$

Operating margin can be a key metric for managers to watch, and not just because many companies tie bonus payments to operating-margin targets. The reason is that nonfinancial managers don't have much control over the other items—interest and taxes—that are ultimately subtracted to get net profit margin. So operating margin is a good indicator of how well managers as a group are doing their jobs. A downward trend line in operating margin should be a flashing yellow light. It shows that costs and expenses are rising faster than sales, which is rarely a healthy sign. As with gross margin, it's easier to see the trends in operating results when you're looking at percentages rather than raw numbers. A percentage change shows not only the direction of the change but how great a change it is.

NET PROFIT MARGIN PERCENTAGE

Net profit margin percentage, or net margin, tells a company how much out of every sales dollar it gets to keep after *everything* else has been paid for—people, vendors, lenders, the government, and so on. It is also known as return on sales, or ROS. Again, it's just net profit divided by revenue, expressed as a percentage:

$$\text{net margin} = \frac{\text{net profit}}{\text{revenue}} = \frac{\$248}{\$8{,}689} = 2.8\%$$

Net profit is the proverbial bottom line, so net margin is a bottom-line ratio. But it's highly variable from one industry to another. Net margin is low in most kinds of retailing, for example. In some kinds of manufacturing it can be relatively high. The best point of comparison for net margin is a company's performance in previous time periods and its performance relative to similar companies in the same industry.

All the ratios we have looked at so far use numbers from the income statement alone. Now we want to introduce some different profitability metrics, which draw from both the income statement and the balance sheet.

RETURN ON ASSETS

Return on assets, or ROA, tells you what percentage of every dollar *invested* in the business was returned to you as profit. This measure isn't quite as intuitive as the ones we already mentioned, but the fundamental idea isn't complex. Every business puts assets to work: cash, facilities, machinery, equipment, vehicles, inventory, whatever. A manufacturing company may have a lot of capital tied up in plant and equipment. A service business may have expensive computer and telecommunications systems. Retailers need a lot of inventory. All these assets show up on the balance sheet. The total assets figure shows how many dollars, in whatever form, are being utilized in the business to generate profit. ROA simply shows how effective the company is at using those assets to generate profit. It's a measure that can be used in any given industry to compare the performance of companies of different size.

The formula (and sample calculation) is simply this:

$$\text{return on assets} = \frac{\text{net profit}}{\text{total assets}} = \frac{\$248}{\$5{,}193} = 4.8\%$$

ROA has another idiosyncrasy by comparison with the income statement ratios mentioned earlier. It's hard for gross margin or net margin to be too high; you generally want to see them as high as possible. But ROA can be too high. An ROA that is considerably above the industry norm may suggest that the company isn't renewing its asset base for the future—that is, it isn't investing in new machinery and equipment. If that's true, its long-term prospects will be compromised, however good its ROA may look at the moment. (In assessing ROA, however, remember that norms vary widely from one industry to another. Service and retail businesses require less in terms of assets than manufacturing companies; then again, they usually generate lower margins.)

Another possibility if ROA is very high is that executives are playing fast and loose with the balance sheet, using various accounting tricks to reduce the asset base and therefore making the ROA look better. Remember

Return on Investment

Why isn't ROI included in our list of profitability ratios? The reason is that the term has a number of different meanings. Traditionally, RO! was the same as ROA: return on assets. But these days it can also mean return on a particular investment. What is the ROI on that machine? What's the ROI on our training program? What's the ROI of our new acquisition? These calculations will be different depending on how people are measuring costs and returns. We'll return to ROI calculations of this sort in part 6.

Enron, the energy-trading company that collapsed in 2001? Enron had set up a host of partnerships partially owned by CFO Andrew Fastow and other executives, and then it "sold" assets to the partnerships. The company's share of the partnerships' profits appeared in its income statement, but the assets were nowhere to be found on its balance sheet. Enron's ROA was great, but Enron wasn't a healthy company.

RETURN ON EQUITY

Return on equity, or ROE, is a little different: it tells us what percentage of profit we make for every dollar of equity invested in the company. Remember the difference between assets and equity: *assets* refers to what the company owns, and *equity* refers to its net worth as determined by accounting rules.

As with the other profitability ratios, ROE can be used to compare a company with its competitors (and, indeed, with companies in other industries). Still, the comparison isn't always simple. For instance, Company A may have a higher ROE than Company B because it has borrowed more money—that is, it has greater liabilities and proportionately less equity invested in the company. Is this good or bad? The answer depends on whether Company A is taking on too much risk or whether, by contrast, it is using borrowed money judiciously to enhance its return. That gets us into ratios such as debt-to-equity, which we'll take up in chapter 22.

At any rate, here are the formula and sample calculation for ROE:

$$\text{return on equity} = \frac{\text{net profit}}{\text{shareholders' equity}} = \frac{\$248}{\$2{,}457} = 10.1\%$$

From an investor's perspective, ROE is a key ratio. Depending on interest rates, an investor can probably earn 2, 3, or 4 percent on a treasury bond, which is about as close to a risk-free investment as you can get. So if someone is going to put money into a company, he'll want a substantially higher return on his equity. ROE doesn't specify how much cash he'll ultimately get out of the company, since that depends on the company's decision about dividend payments and on how much the stock price appreciates until he sells. But it's a good indication of whether the company is even capable of generating a return that is worth whatever risk the investment may entail.

VARIATIONS ON A THEME: RONA, ROTC, ROIC, AND ROCE

Many businesses use somewhat more complex profitability ratios to gauge their performance. These include return on net assets (RONA), return on total capital (ROTC), return on invested capital (ROIC), and return on capital employed (ROCE). Individual businesses use different formulas to calculate these ratios, but they all measure essentially the same thing: how much return the business generated relative to its outside investment and financing. In other words, they answer this question: Did the company earn enough of a profit to justify the amount of "other people's money" it is using?

A generic version of the formula used in calculating these ratios looks like this:

$$\frac{\text{net income before interest on debt and after tax}}{\text{total equity + total interest-bearing debt}}$$

The numerator is often called NOPAT, which stands for *net operating profit after tax*. It shows how much money the company would have made if it (a) had no debt and thus (b) had no interest costs but (c) had to pay taxes on all of its operating profits. (Interest on debt is deductible for tax purposes.)

In the RONA or net assets approach, the denominator is total assets minus all assets financed by non-interest-bearing liabilities, such as accounts payable and accrued expenses. In the ROCE, ROIC, or ROTC approach, shown in the equation above, the denominator is total equity plus all interest-bearing debt. Fundamentally, the various approaches amount to the same thing. You are separating out the liabilities you have to pay interest on from those you don't. The separation reflects the fact that some of the financing necessary to run a business comes from such items as accrued liabilities, accounts payable, and deferred taxes. These will ultimately wind up as charges on the income statement, but the people to whom the money is owed don't expect a return.

Using the sample income statement and balance sheet in the appendix, you can calculate these ratios as follows. We have left out the zeroes for simplicity's sake:

1. Calculate the company's income before taxes. This is just operating income or EBIT less interest expenses: $652 – $191 = $461.

2. Determine the company's tax rate. It shows a charge on the income statement of $213 for taxes, and $213/$461 = 46 percent. This is a bit higher than most US businesses, which usually pay between 30 percent and 40 percent.

3. Determine the tax liability on the company's operating profit: $652 × 46% = $301. NOPAT or net operating profit after tax is $652 – $301 or $351. *This is the numerator of all the ratios.*

4. Calculate the denominator. First add up all the interest-bearing debt on the balance sheet. In this case the category includes the credit line of $100, the current portion of long-term debt of $52, and the long-term debt of $1,037. The total is $1,189. The other liabilities on the balance sheet don't carry interest—though in the real world you might need to study them to make sure that is the case. Usually it is.

5. Now add this figure to total equity: $1,189 + $2,457 = $3,646. This is the all the capital that outsiders have provided plus whatever the company has retained from profits. It is the denominator of the ratio.

6. Finally, calculate the RONA, ROTC, ROIC, or ROCE for this business:

$$\frac{\$351}{\$3,646} = 9.6\%$$

What does it all mean? For every dollar tied up in this company, the return in the past year was 9.6 percent. If the ratio is higher than expected, stakeholders with money in the business are happy. If it is lower, they might want to look elsewhere. These ratios are essential for measuring the return on the business's overall capital.

One note on all such ratios: you'll notice that they compare a profit number taken from the income statement to a capital number taken from the balance sheet. This creates a potential problem: NOPAT represents money earned during an entire year, but the denominator—total capital—is shown for a single point in time, the end of the year. Many financial folks prefer to take an average of several balance sheets during the year to get an "average" total capital figure rather than using just year-end numbers. (See the toolbox at the end of this part for more on this topic.)

Whether you're calculating simple profitability ratios or more complex ones, do remember one thing: the numerator is some form of profit, which is always an estimate. The denominators, too, are based on assumptions and estimates. The ratios are useful, particularly when they are tracked over time to establish trend lines. But we shouldn't be lulled into thinking that they are impervious to artistic effort.

22

Leverage Ratios

The Balancing Act

LEVERAGE RATIOS LET YOU SEE HOW—and how extensively—a company uses debt. *Debt* is a loaded word for many people: it conjures up images of credit cards, interest payments, an enterprise in hock to the bank. But consider the analogy with home ownership. As long as a family takes on a mortgage it can afford, debt allows the family to live in a house that it might otherwise never be able to own. What's more, homeowners can deduct the interest paid on the debt from their taxable income, making it even cheaper to own that house. So it is with a business: debt allows a company to grow beyond what its invested capital alone would allow, and indeed to earn profits that expand its equity base. A business can also deduct interest payments on debt from its taxable income. The financial analyst's word for debt is *leverage*. The implication of the term is that a business can use a modest amount of capital to build up a larger amount of assets through debt to run the business, just the way a person using a lever can move a larger weight than she otherwise could.

The term *leverage* is actually defined in two ways in business—*operating leverage* and *financial leverage*. The ideas are related but different. Operating leverage is the ratio between fixed costs and variable costs; increasing your operating leverage means adding to fixed costs with the objective of reducing variable costs. A retailer that occupies a bigger, more efficient store and a manufacturer that builds a bigger, more productive factory are both increasing their fixed costs. But they hope to reduce their variable costs, because the new collection of assets is more efficient than the old. These are examples of operating leverage. Financial leverage, by contrast, simply means the extent to which a company's asset base is financed by debt.

Leverage of either kind makes it possible for a company to make more money, but it also increases risk. The airline industry is an example of a business with high operating leverage—all those airplanes!—*and* high financial leverage, since most of the planes are financed through debt. The combination creates enormous risk, because if revenue drops off for any reason, the companies are not easily able to cut those fixed costs. That's pretty much what happened after September 11, 2001. The airlines were forced to shut down for a couple of weeks, and the industry lost billions of dollars in just that short time.

Here we will focus only on financial leverage, and we'll look at just two ratios: debt-to-equity and interest coverage.

DEBT-TO-EQUITY

The debt-to-equity ratio is simple and straightforward: it tells how much debt the company has for every dollar of shareholders' equity. The formula and sample calculation look like this:

$$\text{debt-to-equity ratio} = \frac{\text{total liabilities}}{\text{shareholders' equity}} = \frac{\$2{,}736}{\$2{,}457} = 1.11$$

(Note that this ratio isn't usually expressed in percentage terms.) Both these numbers come from the balance sheet.

What's a good debt-to-equity ratio? As with most ratios, the answer depends on the industry. But many, many companies have a debt-to-equity ratio considerably larger than 1—that is, they have more debt than equity. Since the interest on debt is deductible from a company's taxable income, plenty of companies use debt to finance at least a part of their business. In fact, companies with particularly low debt-to-equity ratios may be targets for a leveraged buyout, in which management or other investors use debt to buy up the stock.

Bankers love the debt-to-equity ratio. They use it to determine whether or not to offer a company a loan. They know from experience what a reasonable debt-to-equity ratio is for a company of a given size in a particular industry (and, of course, they check out profitability, cash flow, and other measures as well). For a manager, knowing the debt-to-equity ratio and how it compares with those of competitors is a handy gauge of how senior management is likely to feel about taking on more debt. If the ratio is high, raising more cash through borrowing could be difficult. So expansion could require more equity investment.

INTEREST COVERAGE

Bankers love this one, too. It's a measure of the company's "interest exposure"—how much interest it has to pay every year—relative to how much it's making. The formula and calculation look like this:

$$\text{interest coverage} = \frac{\text{operating profit}}{\text{annual interest charges}} = \frac{\$652}{\$191} = 3.41$$

In other words, the ratio shows how easy it will be for the company to pay its interest. A ratio that gets too close to 1 is obviously a bad sign: most of a company's profit is going to pay off interest! A high ratio is generally a sign that the company can afford to take on more debt—or at least that it can make the payments.

What happens when either of these ratios heads too far in the wrong direction—that is, too high for debt-to-equity and too low for interest coverage? We'd like to think that senior management's response is always to focus on paying off debt, so as to get both ratios back into a reasonable range. But financial artists often have different ideas. There's a wonderful little invention called an *operating lease*, for instance, which is widely used in the airline industry and others. Rather than buying equipment such as an airplane outright, a company leases it from an investor. The lease payments count as an expense on the income statement, but there is no asset and no debt related to that asset on a company's books. Some companies that are already overleveraged are willing to pay a premium to lease equipment just to keep these two ratios in the area that bankers and investors like to see. If you want to get a complete sense of your company's indebtedness, by all means calculate the ratios—but ask someone in finance if the company uses any debtlike instruments such as operating leases as well.

23

Liquidity Ratios

Can We Pay Our Bills?

LIQUIDITY RATIOS TELL YOU about a company's ability to meet all its financial obligations—not just debt but payroll, payments to vendors, taxes, and so on. These ratios are particularly important to small businesses—the ones that are in most danger of running out of cash—but they become important whenever a larger company encounters financial trouble as well. Not to harp on the airlines too much, but several of the larger carriers have been through bankruptcy in recent years. You can bet that professional investors and bondholders have been carefully watching their liquidity ratios ever since.

Again, we'll limit ourselves to two of the most common ratios.

CURRENT RATIO

The current ratio measures a company's current assets against its current liabilities. Remember from the balance sheet chapters (part 3) that *current* in accountantese generally means a period of less than a year. So current assets are those that can be converted into cash in less than a year; the figure normally includes accounts receivable and inventory as well as cash. Current liabilities are those that will have to be paid off in less than a year, mostly accounts payable and short-term loans.

The formula and sample calculation for the current ratio are as follows:

$$\text{current ratio} = \frac{\text{current assets}}{\text{current liabilities}} = \frac{\$2{,}750}{\$1{,}174} = 2.34$$

This is another ratio that can be both too low and too high. In most industries, a current ratio is too low when it is getting close to 1. At that point, you are just barely able to cover the liabilities that will come due with the cash you'll have coming in. Most bankers aren't going to lend money to a company with a current ratio anywhere near 1. Less than 1, of course, is *way* too low, regardless of how much cash you have in the bank. With a current ratio of less than 1, you know you're going to run short of cash sometime during the next year unless you can find a way of generating more cash or attracting more from investors.

A current ratio is too high when it suggests that the company is sitting on its cash rather than investing it or returning it to shareholders. By early 2012, for example, Apple had amassed a cash hoard of nearly $100 billion (yes, *billion*). To the delight of most investors, the company announced in March of that year that it would begin paying shareholders dividends for the first time in many years. Google, at this writing, has a ton of cash in the bank as well. The current ratio at both companies has shot through the ceiling.

QUICK RATIO

The quick ratio is also known as the *acid test*, which gives you an idea of its importance. Here are the formula and calculation:

$$\text{quick ratio} = \frac{\text{current assets} - \text{inventory}}{\text{current liabilities}} = \frac{\$2{,}750 - \$1{,}270}{\$1{,}174} = 1.26$$

Notice that the quick ratio is the current ratio with inventory removed from the calculation. What's the significance of subtracting inventory? Nearly everything else in the current assets category is cash or is easily transformed into cash. Most receivables, for example, will be paid in a month or two, so they're almost as good as cash. The quick ratio shows how easy it would be for a company to pay off its short-term debt without waiting to sell off inventory or convert it into product. Any business that has a lot of cash tied up in inventory has to know that lenders and vendors will be looking at its quick ratio—and will be expecting it (in most cases) to be significantly above 1.

24

Efficiency Ratios

Making the Most of Your Assets

EFFICIENCY RATIOS HELP YOU EVALUATE how efficiently you manage certain key balance sheet assets and liabilities.

The phrase *managing the balance sheet* may have a peculiar ring, especially since most managers are accustomed to focusing only on the income statement. But think about it: the balance sheet lists assets and liabilities, and these assets and liabilities are always in flux. If you can reduce inventory or speed up collection of receivables, you will have a direct and immediate impact on your company's cash position. The efficiency ratios let you know how you're doing on just such measures of performance. (We'll have more to say on managing the balance sheet in part 7.)

INVENTORY DAYS AND TURNOVER

These ratios can be a little confusing. They're based on the fact that inventory flows through a company, and it can flow at a greater or lesser speed. Moreover, how fast it flows matters a lot. If you look at inventory as frozen cash, then the faster you can get it out the door and collect the actual cash, the better off you will be.

So let's begin with a ratio sporting the catchy name *days in inventory*, or DII. (It's also called *inventory days.*) Essentially, it measures the number of days inventory stays in the system. The numerator is average inventory, which is just beginning inventory plus ending inventory (found on the balance sheet for each date) divided by 2. (Some companies use just the ending inventory number.) The denominator is cost of goods sold (COGS) per day, which is a measure of how much inventory is actually used in each day. The formula and sample calculation:

$$\text{DII} = \frac{\text{average inventory}}{\text{COGS/day}} = \frac{(\$1{,}270 + \$1{,}514)/2}{\$6{,}756/360} = 74.2$$

(Financial folks tend to use 360 as the number of days in a year, just because it's a round number.) In this example, inventory stayed in the system for 74.2 days. Whether that's good or bad, of course, depends on the product, the industry, the competition, and so on.

Inventory turns, the other inventory measure, is a measure of how many times inventory turns over in a year. If every item of inventory was processed at exactly the same rate, inventory turns would be the number of times per year you sold out your stock and had to replenish it. The formula and sample calculation are simple:

$$\text{inventory turns} = \frac{360}{\text{DII}} = \frac{360}{74.2} = 4.85$$

In the example, inventory turns over 4.85 times a year. But what are we actually measuring here? Both ratios are a measure of how efficiently a company uses its inventory. The higher the number of inventory turns—or the lower the inventory days—the tighter your management of inventory and the better your cash position. So long as you have enough inventory on hand to meet customer demands, the more efficient you can be, the better. In the four quarters ending in September 2011, Target Stores had inventory turns of 4.9—a fair number for a big retailer. But Walmart's turns were 7.6, much better. In the retail business, a difference in the inventory turnover ratio can mean the difference between success and failure; both Target and Walmart are successful, though Walmart is certainly in the lead. If your responsibilities are anywhere near inventory management, you need to be tracking this ratio carefully. (And even if they aren't, there's nothing to stop you from raising the issue: "Hey, Sally, how come there's been an uptick in our DII recently?") These two ratios are key levers that can be used by financially intelligent managers to create a more efficient organization.

DAYS SALES OUTSTANDING

Days sales outstanding, or DSO, is also known as *average collection period* and *receivable days*. It's a measure of the average time it takes to collect the cash from sales—in other words, how fast customers pay their bills.

The numerator of this ratio, usually, is ending accounts receivable, taken from the balance sheet at the end of the period you're looking at. (Why "usually"? In some circumstances, A/R may spike at the end of a period, so the accountants may then use average A/R as the numerator.) The denominator is revenue per day—just the annual sales figure divided by 360. The formula and sample calculation look like this:

$$\text{days sales outstanding} = \frac{\text{ending A/R}}{\text{revenue/day}} = \frac{\$1{,}312}{\$8{,}689/360} = 54.4$$

In other words, it takes this company's customers an average of about fifty-four days to pay their bills.

Right there, of course, is an avenue for rapid improvement in a company's cash position. Why is it taking so long? Are customers unhappy because of product defects or poor service? Are salespeople too lax in negotiating terms? Are the receivables clerks demoralized or inefficient? Is everybody laboring with outdated financial management software? DSO does tend to vary a good deal by industry, region, economy, and seasonality, but still: if this company could get the ratio down to forty-five or even forty days, it would improve its cash position considerably. This is a prime example of a significant phenomenon; namely, that careful management can improve a business's financial picture even with no change in its revenues or costs.

DSO is also a key ratio for the folks who are doing due diligence on a potential acquisition. A high DSO may be a red flag in that it suggests that customers aren't paying their bills in a timely fashion. Maybe the customers themselves are in financial trouble. Maybe the target company's operations and financial management are poor. Maybe there is some fast-and-loose financial artistry going on. We'll come back to DSO in part 7 on the management of working capital; for the moment, note only that it is by definition a weighted average. So it's important that the due diligence folks look at the aging of receivables—that is, how old specific invoices are and how many there are. It may be that a couple of unusually large and unusually late invoices are skewing the DSO number.

DAYS PAYABLE OUTSTANDING

The days payable outstanding (DPO) ratio shows the average number of days it takes a company to pay its own outstanding invoices. It's sort of the flip side of DSO. The formula is similar: take ending accounts payable and divide by COGS per day:

$$\text{days payable outstanding} = \frac{\text{ending A/P}}{\text{COGS/day}} = \frac{\$1{,}022}{\$6{,}756/360} = 54.5$$

In other words, this company's suppliers are waiting a *long* time to get paid—about as long as the company is taking to collect its receivables.

So what? Isn't that the vendors' problem to worry about, rather than this company's managers? Well, yes and no. The higher the DPO, the better a company's cash position, but the less happy its vendors are likely to be. A company with a reputation for slow pay may find that top-of-the-line vendors don't compete for its business quite so aggressively as they otherwise might. Prices might be a little higher, terms a little stiffer. A company with a reputation for prompt thirty-day payment will find the exact opposite. Watching DPO is a way of ensuring that the company is sticking to whatever balance it wants to strike between preserving its cash and keeping vendors happy.

PROPERTY, PLANT, AND EQUIPMENT TURNOVER

This ratio tells you how many dollars of sales your company gets for each dollar invested in property, plant, and equipment (PPE). It's a measure of how efficient you are at generating revenue from fixed assets such as buildings, vehicles, and machinery. The calculation is simply total revenue (from the income statement) divided by ending PPE (from the balance sheet):

$$\text{PPE turnover} = \frac{\text{revenue}}{\text{PPE}} = \frac{\$8,689}{\$2,230} = 3.90$$

By itself, \$3.90 of sales for every dollar of PPE doesn't mean much. But it may mean a lot when compared with past performance and with competitors' performance. A company that generates a lower PPE turnover, other things being equal, isn't using its assets as efficiently as a company with a higher one. So check the trend lines and the industry averages to see how your company stacks up.

But please note that sneaky little qualifier, "other things being equal." The fact is, this is one ratio where the art of finance can affect the numbers dramatically. If a company leases much of its equipment rather than owning it, for instance, the leased assets may not show up on its balance sheet. Its apparent asset base will be that much lower and PPE turnover that much higher. Some companies pay bonuses pegged to this ratio, which gives managers an incentive to lease equipment rather than buy it. Leasing may or may not make strategic sense for any individual enterprise. What doesn't make sense is to have the decision made on the basis of a bonus payment. Incidentally, a lease must meet specific requirements to qualify as an operating lease (which may not show up on the balance sheet) as opposed to a capital lease (which does). Check with your finance department before entering into any kind of lease.

TOTAL ASSET TURNOVER

This is the same idea as the previous ratio, but it compares revenue with total assets, not just fixed assets. (Total assets, remember, includes cash, receivables, and inventory as well as PPE and other long-term assets.) The formula and calculations:

$$\text{total asset turnover} = \frac{\text{revenue}}{\text{total assets}} = \frac{\$8,689}{\$5,193} = 1.67$$

Total asset turnover gauges not just efficiency in the use of fixed assets, but efficiency in the use of all assets. If you can reduce inventory, total asset turnover rises. If you can cut average receivables, total asset turnover rises.

If you can increase sales while holding assets constant (or increasing at a slower rate), total asset turnover rises. Any of these managing-the-balance-sheet moves improves efficiency. Watching the trends in total asset turnover shows you how you're doing.

There are many more ratios than these, of course. Financial professionals of all sorts use a lot of them. Investment analysts do, too, as we'll see in chapter 25. Your own organization is likely to have specific ratios that are appropriate for the company, the industry, or both. You'll want to learn how to calculate them, how to use them, and how you affect them. But those we have outlined here are the most common for most working managers.

25

The Investor's Perspective

The "Big Five" Numbers and Shareholder Value

AS WE'VE MENTIONED BEFORE, we wrote this book for people who work in organizations, not for investors. But the investor's perspective always informs managerial decisions, because every company must do its best to keep shareholders and bondholders happy. Even the owners and employees of privately held companies can benefit from understanding this perspective, since it provides some good indicators of the financial health of their company. So this chapter addresses the question: which ratios and other indicators does the typical investor or bondholder care most about?

In our view, Wall Street and other outside investors are really looking at five key metrics when they assess a company's financial performance or its attractiveness as an investment. You can think of these measures as the Big Five. When all five are moving in the right direction, it's a safe bet that investors will favor the company's prospects.

The Big Five are:

- Revenue growth from one year to the next
- Earnings per share (EPS)
- Earnings before interest, taxes, depreciation, and amortization (EBITDA)

- Free cash flow (FCF)
- Return on total capital (ROTC) or return on equity (ROE). ROE is the right metric for financial businesses such as banks and insurance companies.

Let's briefly look at each one.

REVENUE GROWTH YEAR OVER YEAR

Not every company grows. Most small businesses reach a certain size and stay there because the opportunities for growth are limited. Some privately held companies have terrific growth prospects, but the owners decide that they prefer to keep the business relatively small. (A great book called *Small Giants*, by Bo Burlingham, tells the story of many such companies.[1]) But when a business "goes public"—sells stock to outside investors—it has no choice about whether to pursue growth. Investors won't buy the stock unless they expect the value of their investment to increase over time. They want to see a growing dividend, an appreciating stock price, or both. To provide either one, the company must expand its business.

How much growth is reasonable? It depends on the company, the industry, and the economic situation. Some high-tech companies—Google is an example—go through periods of explosive growth. Most growth-oriented companies expand far more slowly; a growth rate of 10 percent a year, sustained over time, is remarkably good. (According to research by Bain & Company, only about 10 percent of global companies sustain an annual growth rate in revenue and earnings of at least 5.5 percent over ten years while also earning their cost of capital.[2]) Some large companies peg their goals to the growth in gross domestic product (GDP) in the countries where they operate. General Electric, for instance, typically plans to expand its business by two or three times the rate of GDP growth. If GDP is increasing at 1 percent and GE grows at 2 or 3 percent, the company can declare victory.

EARNINGS PER SHARE

EPS is often the first number companies report to investors in their quarterly earnings calls. It is simply the company's net income for the quarter or year divided by the average number of shares outstanding during the period.

Investors expect increases in EPS over time, just as they do with revenue. Other things being equal, a growing EPS presages an increasing stock price. During an economic slowdown, revenues might fall, but most companies try hard to keep EPS up by reducing costs. Shareholders can accept revenue declines during a slump, but they don't like to see a drop in EPS.

EARNINGS BEFORE INTEREST, TAXES, DEPRECIATION, AND AMORTIZATION

We've already mentioned EBITDA a few times in this book. It's an important measure because investors and bankers view it as a good indicator of future operating cash flow. Lenders like it because it can help them assess a company's ability to repay its loans. Shareholders like it because it is a measure of cash earnings before the accountants have added in noncash expenses such as depreciation. EBITDA can be manipulated by accounting tricks, as we noted earlier, but it isn't as easily manipulated as net profit. A strong, healthy company should experience growth in EBITDA over time.

Incidentally, EBITDA is often used in valuing businesses. Many companies are bought and sold at a price that is an agreed-upon multiple of EBITDA.

FREE CASH FLOW

We discussed free cash flow in the toolbox for part 4. It's a key part of any investor's measurement kit. If a company's free cash flow is healthy and growing, investors can be pretty sure that it is doing well and that its stock price will rise over time. Moreover, a company with a healthy free cash flow can finance its own growth even when investment or debt capital is hard to come by.

Here's one more wrinkle on these two indicators: many investors are now looking at free cash flow *divided* by EBITDA. When that ratio is low, it may indicate that the company is trying to make its EBITDA look strong through accounting gimmickry even though its cash flow is relatively weak. Some people call this ratio the *cash conversion metric*. Another formula that's sometimes used is operating cash flow divided by EBIT (rather than by EBITDA). Either way, the metric shows how well the company is converting profit to cash.

RETURN ON TOTAL CAPITAL OR RETURN ON EQUITY

ROTC, discussed in chapter 21, tells investors whether the business is generating a return high enough to justify their investment. ROE is most commonly used in evaluating financial businesses. A bank, for instance, makes money by borrowing money in the form of deposits and then lending those deposits out. ROTC isn't a good indicator of its performance because a bank's debt to its depositors is part of its business, not part of its capital. ROE is a far better gauge of performance.

MARKET CAP, PRICE-TO-EARNINGS, AND SHAREHOLDER VALUE

Along with the Big Five, investors also examine many other ratios and indicators. Three of the most common are market capitalization, the price-to-earnings ratio (P/E), and what is often called *shareholder value*.

A company's *market cap* is simply the current stock price of a company multiplied by the number of shares outstanding. It represents the total value of the business on any given day. If a company has 10 million shares outstanding and its market price on Tuesday is $20, its market cap that day is $200 million. Many large companies have market caps well over $100 billion. At the end of 2011, Apple's was about $375 billion, IBM's close to $220 billion.

While the market cap shows what a company is worth to investors, the book value of the company is simply the value of the equity of the business as shown on the balance sheet. Most companies' market caps are significantly higher than their book values. Some investors—Warren Buffett, for example—like to look at the "market to book" ratio. Buffett often tries to find companies that are trading at a market cap close to or even below their book value.

The *price-to-earnings ratio* or P/E is the current stock price divided by the prior year's earning per share. Historically, most businesses have traded in public markets at P/E ratios of roughly 16 to 18. Companies with higher ratios are considered to have high growth potential; those with lower ratios are considered slow-growth businesses. Investors often try to find companies with P/E ratios lower than the investor believes appropriate. At the end of 2011 both Apple and IBM had a P/E of about 14.6.

In a sense, all these measures are indicators of a company's shareholder value. But the term "shareholder value" crops up in a number of different contexts and has a variety of meanings. Sometimes it just means market cap; sometimes it refers to the expected future cash flows of a company (which, after all, is what investors are buying when they purchase a share of stock); sometimes it refers to the increase in dividends, share price, or both that investors hope to realize over time. A CEO might write in his annual letter, "Our goal is to increase shareholder value." It hardly matters what definition he is using, because increases in any one of them would redound to investors' advantage.

Increasing shareholder value is important to everyone who works for a company, not just to shareholders. A higher shareholder value compared with the past or compared with competitors bespeaks relative financial strength. Lenders like to lend to strong companies. Investors like to invest in them. Strong companies are more likely than weaker ones to survive tough economic times and to prosper in good ones. They are more likely to offer their employees job security and opportunities for advancement, to say nothing of steady paychecks and annual raises. Customers like strong companies as well. Strong companies have more pricing flexibility than weak ones, and they are likely to be around next month and next year.

What determines shareholder value? It isn't just current financial performance. A well-regarded biotech company, for instance, may have a high market cap even though it has no earnings, just because investors expect it to create a lot of value in the future through the products it brings to market. Conversely, a solidly profitable company with poor growth prospects may be worth considerably less than a company with lower current profits and better hopes for the future.

In general, shareholder value depends on market perceptions, which in turn are driven by:

- The company's current financial performance
- The company's prospects for growth in the future
- The company's anticipated cash flows in the future
- The predictability of its performance—that is, the degree of risk involved
- Investors' assessments of the expertise of a company's management and the skills of its employees . . .

. . . and of course a lot of other factors, such as the overall state of the economy, the condition of the stock market in general, the level of speculative fervor, and so on. At any given point in time, investors will disagree about a company's "true" value, which is why some are willing to buy shares at a particular price and some are willing to sell them.

Sophisticated investors always look at the kinds of accounting measures we describe in this book: sales, cost of sales, operating margin, and so on. They look at a company's physical assets, its inventories, its receivables, its level of overhead, and many other indicators. But they also understand that investment is a game of psychology as well as of economics. As the economist John Maynard Keynes once pointed out, buying stocks is like trying to anticipate who will win a beauty contest. You want to choose not the person who you think is the most beautiful but the person you think *everyone else* will see as most beautiful. So it is with stocks: prices rise not just when a company turns in great performance but when a lot of investors believe that the future will bring even better performance

We hope that you now see the importance of ratios, from both a manager's and an investor's perspective. Although understanding the financial statements is important, it is just a start on the journey to financial intelligence. Ratios take you to the next level; they give you a way to read between (or maybe underneath) the lines, so you can really understand what is going on. They are a useful tool for analyzing your company or any other company, and for telling its financial story.

Part Five
Toolbox

WHICH RATIOS ARE MOST IMPORTANT TO *YOUR* BUSINESS?

Certain ratios are generally seen as critical in certain industries. Retailers, for instance, watch inventory turnover closely. The faster they can turn their stock, the more efficient use they are making of their other assets, such as the store itself. But individual companies typically like to create their own key ratios, depending on their circumstances and competitive situation. For example, Joe's company, Setpoint, is a small, project-based business that must keep a careful eye on both operating expenses and cash. So which ratios do Setpoint's managers watch most closely? One is homegrown: gross profit divided by operating expenses. Keeping an eye on that ratio ensures that operating expenses don't get out of line in relation to the gross profit dollars the company is generating. The other is the current ratio, which compares current assets with current liabilities. The current ratio is usually a good indication of whether a company has enough cash to meet its obligations.

You may already know your company's key ratios. If not, try asking the CFO or someone on her staff what they are. We bet they'll be able to answer the question pretty easily.

THE POWER OF PERCENT OF SALES

You'll often see one kind of ratio built right into a company's income statement: each line item will be expressed not only in dollars but as a percent of sales. For instance, COGS might be 68 percent of sales, operating expenses 20 percent, and so on. The percent-of-sales figure itself will be tracked over time to establish trend lines. Companies can pursue this analysis in some detail—for example, tracking what percent of sales each product line accounts for, or what percent of sales each store or region in a retail chain accounts for. The power here is that percent-of-sales calculations give a manager much more information than the raw numbers alone. Percent of sales allows a manager to track his expenses in relationship to sales. Otherwise, it's tough for the manager to know if he is in line or not as sales increase and decrease.

If your company doesn't break out percent of sales, try this exercise: locate the last three income statements and calculate percent of sales for each major line item. Then track the results over time. If you see certain items creep up while others creep down, ask yourself why that happened—and if you don't know, try to find someone who does. The exercise can teach you a lot about the competitive (or other) pressures your company has been under.

RATIO RELATIONSHIPS

Like the financial statements themselves, ratios fit together mathematically. We won't go into enormous detail here, because this book isn't aimed at financial professionals. But one relationship among ratios is worth spelling out because it shows so clearly what we have been saying; namely, that managers can affect a business's performance in a variety of ways.

Start with the fact that one of a business's key profitability objectives is return on assets, or ROA. That's a critical metric because investment capital is a business's fuel, and if a company can't deliver a satisfactory ROA, its flow of capital will dry up. We know from this part that ROA is equal to net income divided by total assets.

But another way to express ROA is through two different factors that, multiplied together, equal net income divided by total assets. Here they are:

$$\frac{\text{net income}}{\text{revenue}} \times \frac{\text{revenue}}{\text{assets}} = \frac{\text{net income}}{\text{assets}} = \text{ROA}$$

The first term, net income divided by revenue, is of course net profit margin percentage, or return on sales (ROS). The second term, revenue divided by assets, is asset turnover, discussed in chapter 24. So net profit margin times asset turnover equals ROA.

The equation shows explicitly that there are two moves to the hoop, where the "hoop" is higher ROA. One is to increase net profit margin, either by raising prices or by delivering goods or services more efficiently. That can be tough if the marketplace you operate in is highly competitive. A second is to increase the asset turnover ratio. That opens up another set of possible actions: reducing average inventory, reducing days sales outstanding, and reducing the purchase of property, plant, and equipment. If you can't improve your net profit margin, working on those objectives—that is, managing the balance sheet—may be your best path to beating the competition and improving your ROA.

DIFFERENT COMPANIES, DIFFERENT CALCULATIONS

Having read the chapters in this part, you might assume that the formulas we present are "the" formulas. Return on assets, for example, is just net income divided by assets, right? Not necessarily. We have presented the standard formulas, but even with those, companies may decide on a particular way of calculating some of the numbers. The accountants do need to be consistent from one year to the next, and public companies must disclose how they are calculating the ratios. But when you compare one company's ratios with another's, you need to ask whether they are calculating each ratio the same way.

The most common differences arise with balance sheet data. Let's use the same example, return on assets. The denominator, total assets, comes from the balance sheet. Of course, the balance sheet typically shows two points in time, say December 31, 2011, and December 31, 2012. For the standard formula, you use the total assets number from the most recent point in time, December 31, 2012. (This is also called *ending assets*, as it is the last point in time for which you have data.)

But some companies don't believe that one point in time is a good way of measuring total assets. So they might use "average" total assets, adding the 2011 and the 2012 figures and dividing by 2. Or they might calculate a "rolling average" using three, four, or even five quarters of data. As a new quarter closes, they replace the oldest data with the newest in the calculation.

Does it matter? A little. Rolling averages tend to smooth results out, and ending often shows more ups and downs. Then, too, most financial analysts would agree that some kind of averaging makes more sense for calculations such as ROA. As we mentioned in chapter 21, you have an apples-and-oranges situation whenever you compare an income statement number such as net income to a balance sheet number such as total assets. The income statement measures profit or income over a period of time. The balance sheet lists assets at a point in time. So it seems more reasonable to use a rolling average of total assets over the whole period rather than assets at a single point in time.

In general, though, the precise methodology may not matter much. Remember that ratios are used to look at trends over time, and as long as a company's methodology is consistent you can learn a lot from the comparison.

Part Six

How to Calculate (and Really Understand) Return on Investment

26

The Building Blocks of ROI

FINANCIAL INTELLIGENCE is all about understanding how the financial side of business works and how financial decisions are made. The principles discussed in this chapter are the foundation of how some decisions—those relating to capital investment—are made in corporate America.

Most of us need little introduction to the fundamental principle of finance known as the *time value of money*. The reason is that we take advantage of it every day in our personal finances. We take out home mortgages and car loans. We run up balances on our credit cards. Meanwhile, we're putting our own savings into interest-bearing checking or savings accounts, money-market funds, treasury bills, stocks and I bonds, and probably half a dozen other kinds of investments. The United States in particular is a nation of borrowers—in fact, the US government borrowed so much that its debt was downgraded in 2011—but it is also a nation of savers, lenders, and investors. Since all these activities reflect the time value of money, it's a safe bet that most of us have a gut-level understanding of the idea. Those who don't are likely to wind up on the losing end of the principle, which can be expensive indeed.

At its simplest, the principle of the time value of money says this: a dollar in your hand today is worth more than a dollar you expect to collect tomorrow—and it's worth a whole lot more than a dollar you hope to collect ten years from now. The reasons are obvious. You know you have today's dollar, whereas a dollar you expect to get tomorrow (let alone in ten years) is a little iffy. There's risk involved. What's more, you can buy something today with the dollar you have. If you want to spend the dollar you hope to have, you have to wait until you have it. Given the time value of money, anyone who lends money to somebody else expects to be paid interest, and anybody who borrows money expects to pay interest. The longer the time period and the higher the risk, the larger the interest charges are likely to be.

The principle here is the same, of course, even if *interest* isn't the term used and even if there is no fixed expectation about what the return will be. Say you buy stock in a high-tech start-up. You're not going to get any interest, and you probably will never receive a dividend—but you hope you can sell the stock for more than you paid for it. In effect, you're lending the company your money with the expectation of a return on your investment. When and if the return materializes, you can calculate it in percentage terms just as if it were really interest.

This is the basic principle that underlies a business's decisions about capital investments, which we will discuss in this part. The business has to spend cash that it has now in hopes of realizing a return at some future date. If you are charged with preparing a financial proposal for buying a new machine or opening a new branch office—tasks that we'll show you how to do in the following pages—you will be relying on calculations involving the time value of money.

While the time value of money is the basic principle, the three key concepts you'll be using in analyzing capital expenditures are *future value*, *present value*, and *required rate of return*. You may find them confusing at first, but none of them is too complicated. They're simply ways to calculate the time value of money. If you can understand these concepts and use them in your decision making, you'll find yourself thinking more creatively—maybe we should say more artistically—about financial matters, just the way the pros do.

FUTURE VALUE

Future value is what a given amount of cash will be worth in the future if it is loaned out or invested. In personal finance, it's a concept often used in retirement planning. Perhaps you have $50,000 in the bank at age thirty-five, and you want to know what that $50,000 will be worth at age sixty-five. That's the future value of the $50,000. In business, an investment analyst might project the value of a company's stock in two years if earnings grow at some given percent a year. That future-value calculation can help her advise clients as to whether the company is a good investment.

Figuring future value offers a broad canvas for financial artists. Look at that retirement plan, for example. Do you assume an average 3 percent return over the next thirty years, or do you assume an average 6 percent? The difference is substantial: at 3 percent your $50,000 will grow to slightly more than $121,000 (and never mind what inflation will have done to the value of a dollar in the meantime). At 6 percent it will grow to more than $287,000, though with the same caveat about the effect of inflation. It's tough to decide the right interest rate to use: how on earth can anyone know what interest rates will prevail over the next thirty years? At best, calculating future value that far out is educated guesswork—an exercise in artistry.

The investment analyst is in a somewhat better position, because she is looking out only two years. Still, she has more variables to contend with. *Why* does she think earnings might grow at 3 percent or 5 percent or 7 percent or some other rate entirely? And what happens if they do? If earnings grow at only 3 percent, for instance, investors might lose interest and sell their shares, and the stock's price-to-earnings ratio might decline. If earnings grow at 7 percent, investors might get excited, buy more stock, and push up that ratio. And of course, the market itself will have an effect on the stock's price, and nobody can reliably predict the market's overall direction. Again, we're back to educated guesswork.

In fact, every calculation of future value involves a series of assumptions about what will happen between now and the time that you're looking at. Change the assumptions, and you get a different future value. The variance in return rates is a form of financial risk. The longer the investment outlook, the more estimating is required, hence the higher the risk.

PRESENT VALUE

This is the concept used most often in analyzing capital expenditures. It's the reverse of future value. Say you believe that a particular investment will generate $100,000 in cash flow per year over the next three years. If you want to know whether the investment is worth spending money on, you need to know what that $300,000 would be worth right now. Just as you use a particular interest rate to figure future value, you also use an interest rate to "discount" a future value and bring it back to present value. To take a simple example, the present value of $106,000 one year from now at 6 percent interest is $100,000. We are back to the notion that a dollar today is worth more than a dollar tomorrow. In this example, $106,000 in twelve months is worth $100,000 today.

Present-value concepts are widely used to evaluate investments in equipment, real estate, business opportunities, even mergers and acquisitions. But you can see the art of finance clearly here as well. To figure present value, you have to make assumptions *both* about the cash the investment will generate in the future *and* about what kind of an interest rate should be used to discount that future value.

REQUIRED RATE OF RETURN

When you're figuring what interest rate to use in calculating present value, remember that you're working backward. You are assuming your investment will pay off a certain amount in the future, and you want to know how much is worth investing now in order to get that amount at a future date. So your decision about the interest or discount rate is essentially a decision about what interest rate you *need* in order to make the investment at all. You might not invest $100,000 now to get $102,000 in a year—a 2 percent rate—but you might very well invest $100,000 now to get $120,000 in a year—a 20 percent rate. Different companies set the bar, or "hurdle," at different points, and they typically set it higher for riskier projects than for less risky ones. The rate that they require before they will make an investment is called the *required rate of return*, or the "hurdle rate."

There is always some judgment involved in establishing a hurdle rate, but the judgment isn't wholly arbitrary. One factor is the *opportunity cost* involved. The company has only so much cash, and it has to make judgments about how best to use its funds. That 2 percent return is unattractive because the company could probably do better just by buying a treasury bill, which might pay 3 percent or 4 percent with almost no risk. The

20 percent return may well be attractive—it's hard to make 20 percent on most investments—but it obviously depends on how risky the venture is. A second factor is the company's own *cost of capital*. If it borrows money, it has to pay interest. If it uses shareholders' capital, the shareholders expect a return. The proposed investment has to add enough value to the company that debtholders can be repaid and shareholders kept happy. An investment that returns less than the company's cost of capital won't meet these two objectives—so the required rate of return should always be higher than the cost of capital. (See the toolbox at the end of this part for a detailed discussion of cost of capital.)

That said, decisions about hurdle rates are rarely a matter of following a formula. The company's CFO or treasurer will evaluate how risky a given investment is, how it is likely to be financed, and what the company's overall situation is. He knows that shareholders expect the company to invest for the future. He knows, too, that shareholders expect those investments to generate a return at least comparable to what they can get elsewhere at a similar level of risk. He knows—or at least you hope he does—how tight the company's cash position is, how much risk the CEO and the board are comfortable with, and what's going on in the marketplace the company operates in. Then he makes judgments—assumptions—about what kind of hurdle rates make sense. High-growth companies typically use a high hurdle rate, because they must invest their money where they think it will generate the level of growth they need. More stable, low-growth companies typically use a lower hurdle rate. If you don't already know it, someone in your finance organization can tell you what hurdle rate your company uses for the kind of projects you're likely to be involved in.

Opportunity Cost

In everyday language, this phrase denotes what you had to give up to follow a certain course of action. If you spend all your money on a fancy vacation, the opportunity cost is that you can't buy a car. In business, opportunity cost often means the potential benefit forgone from not following the financially optimal course of action.

A word on the calculations involving these concepts. In chapter 27, we'll show you a formula or two. But you don't need to work it all out by hand; you can use a financial calculator, find a book of tables, or just go online. For instance, type "future value calculator" into Google, and you'll get several sites where you can figure simple future values. To be sure, real-world calculations aren't always so easy. Maybe you think the investment you're considering will generate $100,000 in cash in the first year and 3 percent more in each of the subsequent years. Now you have to figure the increase, make assumptions about whether the appropriate discount rate should change from one year to the next, and so forth. Nonfinancial managers generally don't have to worry about actually doing these more complex calculations; the finance folks will do them for you. Usually, they'll have a spreadsheet or template with the appropriate formulas embedded, so that you or they can just plug in the numbers. But you do have to be aware of the concepts and assumptions that they'll use in the process. If you're just plugging in numbers without understanding the logic, you won't understand why the results turn out as they do, and you won't know how to make them turn out differently by starting with different assumptions.

Now let's put these concepts to work.

27

Figuring ROI

The Nitty-Gritty

CAPITAL EXPENDITURES. Cap-ex. Capital investments. Capital budgeting. And of course, return on investment—ROI. Many companies use these terms loosely or even interchangeably, but they're usually referring to the same thing; namely, the process of deciding what capital investments to make to improve the value of the company.

ANALYZING CAPITAL EXPENDITURES

Capital expenditures are large projects that require a significant investment of cash. Every organization defines *significant* differently; some draw the line at $1,000, others at $5,000 or more. Capital expenditures go toward items and projects expected to help generate revenue for more than a year. The category is broad. It includes equipment purchases, business expansions, acquisitions, and the development of new products. A new marketing campaign can be considered a capital expenditure. So can the renovation of a building, the upgrade of a computer system, and the purchase of a new company car.

Companies treat expenditures like these differently from ordinary purchases of inventory, supplies, utilities, and so on, for at least three reasons.

One is that the expenditures involve large (and sometimes indeterminate) amounts of cash. A second is that they are typically expected to provide returns for several years, so the time value of money comes into play. A third is that they always entail some degree of risk. A company may not know whether the expenditure will "work"—that is, whether it will deliver the expected results. Even if it does work generally as planned, the company can't know exactly how much cash the investment will actually help to generate.

We will outline the basic steps of analyzing capital expenditures, and then describe the three methods finance people generally use for calculating whether a given expenditure is worth making. But please: remember that this, too, is an exercise in the art of finance. It's actually kind of amazing; financial professionals can and do analyze proposed projects and make recommendations using a host of assumptions and estimates, and the results turn out well. They even enjoy the challenge of taking these unknowns and quantifying them in a way that makes their company more successful.

With a little financial intelligence, you can contribute your own specialized knowledge to this process. We know of a company where the CFO makes a point of involving engineers and technicians in the capital budgeting process, precisely because they are likely to know more about what an investment in a steel-fabricating plant, say, will actually produce. The CFO likes to say that he'd rather teach those people a little finance than learn metallurgy himself.

So here's how to go about it:

- Step 1 in analyzing a capital expenditure is to *determine the initial cash outlay*. Even this step involves estimates and assumptions: you must make judgments about what a machine or project is likely to cost before it begins to generate revenue. The costs may include purchasing equipment, installing it, allowing people time to learn to use it, and so on. Typically, most of the costs are incurred during the first year, but some may spill over into year two or even year three. All these calculations should be done in terms of cash out the door, not in terms of decreased profits.

- Step 2 is to *project future cash flows* from the investment. (Again, you want to know cash inflows, not profit. We'll have more to say on this distinction later in the chapter.) This is a tricky step—definitely an example of the art of finance—both because it is so difficult to predict the future and because there are many factors that need to be taken into account. (See the toolbox at the end of this part.) Managers need to be conservative, even cautious, in projecting future cash flows from an investment. If the investment returns more than projected, everybody will be happy. If it returns significantly less, no one will be happy, and the company may well have wasted its money.

- Step 3, finally, is to *evaluate the future cash flows*—to figure the return on investment. Are they substantial enough so that the investment is worthwhile? On what basis can we make that determination? Finance professionals typically use three different methods—alone or in combination—for deciding whether a given expenditure is worth it: the payback method, the net present value (NPV) method, and the internal rate of return (IRR) method. Each provides different information, and each has its characteristic strengths and weaknesses.

You can see right away that most of the work and intelligence in good capital budgeting involves the estimates of costs and returns. A lot of data must be collected and analyzed—a tough job in and of itself. Then the data has to be translated into projections about the future. Financially savvy managers will understand that both of these are difficult processes, and will ask questions and challenge assumptions.

LEARNING THE THREE METHODS

To help you see these steps in action and understand how they work, we'll take a very simple example. Your company is considering buying a $3,000 piece of equipment—a specialized computer, say, that will help one of your employees deliver a service to your customers in less time. The computer is expected to last three years. At the end of each of the three years, the cash flow from this piece of equipment is estimated at $1,300. Your company's required rate of return—the hurdle rate—is 8 percent. Do you buy this computer or not?

Payback Method

The payback method is probably the simplest way to evaluate the future cash flow from a capital expenditure. It measures the time required for the cash flow from the project to return the original investment—in other words, it tells you how long it will take to get your money back. The payback period obviously has to be shorter than the life of the project; otherwise, there's no reason to make the investment at all. In our example, you just take the initial investment of $3,000 and divide by the cash flow per year to get the payback period:

$$\frac{\$3{,}000}{\$1{,}300/\text{year}} = 2.31 \text{ years}$$

Since we know the machine will last three years, the payback period meets the first test: it is shorter than the life of the project. What we have not yet calculated is how much cash the project will return over its entire life.

Right there you can see both the strengths and the weaknesses of the payback method. On the plus side, it is simple to calculate and explain. It provides a quick and easy reality check. If a project you are considering has a payback period that is obviously longer than the life of the project, you probably need to look no further. If it has a quicker payback period, you're probably justified in doing some more investigation. This is the method often used in meetings to quickly determine if a project is worth exploring.

On the minus side, the payback method doesn't tell you much. A company doesn't just want to break even on an investment, after all; it wants to generate a return. This method doesn't consider the cash flow beyond breakeven, and it doesn't give you an overall return. Nor does the method consider the time value of money. The method compares the cash outlay today with projected cash flows tomorrow, but it is really comparing cantaloupes to cabbages, because dollars today have a different value than dollars down the road.

For these reasons, payback should be used only to *compare* projects (so that you know which will return the initial investment sooner) or to *reject* projects (those that will never cover their initial investment). But remember, both numbers used in the calculation are estimates. The art in this is pulling the numbers together—how close can you come to quantifying an unknown?

So the payback method is a rough rule of thumb, not strong financial analysis. If payback looks promising, go on to the next method to see if the investment is really worth making.

Net Present Value Method

The net present value method is more complex than payback, but it's also more powerful; indeed, it's usually the finance professional's first choice for analyzing capital expenditures. The reasons? One, it takes into account the time value of money, discounting future cash flows to obtain their value right now. Two, it considers a business's cost of capital or other hurdle rate. Three, it provides an answer in today's dollars, thus allowing you to compare the initial cash outlay with the present value of the return.

How to compute present value? As we mentioned, the actual calculation can be done on a financial calculator, your finance department's spreadsheet, or online with one of the many available Web tools. You can also look up the answer in the present value/future value tables found in finance textbooks. But we'll also show you what the actual formula—it's called the *discounting equation*—looks like, so you can look "underneath" the result and really know what it means.

The discounting equation looks like this:

$$PV = \frac{FV_1}{(1+i)} + \frac{FV_2}{(1+i)^2} + \ldots \frac{FV_n}{(1+i)^n}$$

where:

PV = present value

FV = projected cash flow for each time period

i = discount or hurdle rate

n = number of time periods you're looking at

Net present value is equal to present value minus the initial cash outlay.

For the example we mentioned, the calculation would look like this:

$$PV = \frac{\$1{,}300}{1.08} + \frac{\$1{,}300}{(1.08)^2} + \frac{\$1{,}300}{(1.08)^3} = \$3{,}350$$

and

$$NPV = \$3{,}350 - \$3{,}000 = \$350$$

In words, the total expected cash flow of $3,900 is worth only $3,350 in today's dollars when discounted at 8 percent. Subtract the initial cash outlay of $3,000, and you get an NPV of $350.

How should you interpret this? If the NPV of a project is greater than zero, it should be accepted, because the return is greater than the company's hurdle rate. Here, the return of $350 shows you that the project has a return greater than 8 percent.

Some companies may expect you to run an NPV calculation using more than one discount rate. If you do, you'll see the following relationship:

- As the interest rate increases, NPV decreases.
- As the interest rate decreases, NPV increases.

This relationship holds because higher interest rates mean a higher opportunity cost for funds. If a treasurer sets the hurdle rate at 20 percent, it means she's pretty confident she can get almost that much elsewhere for similar levels of risk. The new investment will have to be pretty darn good to pry loose any funds. By contrast, if she can get only 4 percent elsewhere, many new investments may start to look good. Just as the Federal Reserve stimulates the national economy by lowering interest rates, a company can stimulate internal investment by lowering its hurdle rate. (Of course, it may not be wise policy to do so.)

One drawback of the NPV method is that it can be hard to explain and present to others. Payback is easy to understand, but net present value is a number that's based on the *discounted value of future cash flows*—not a phrase that trips easily off the nonfinancial tongue. Still, a manager who wants to make an NPV presentation should persist. Assuming that the hurdle rate is equal to or greater than the company's cost of capital, *any* investment that passes the net present value test will increase shareholder value, and *any* investment that fails would (if carried out anyway) actually hurt the company and its shareholders.

Another potential drawback—the art of finance, again—is simply that NPV calculations are based on so many estimates and assumptions. The cash flow projections can only be estimated. The initial cost of a project may be hard to pin down. And different discount rates, of course, can give you radically different NPV results. Still, the more you understand about the method, the more you can question somebody else's assumptions—and the easier it will be to prepare your own proposals, using assumptions that you can defend. Your financial intelligence also will be clear to others—your boss, your CEO, whoever—when you present and explain NPV in a meeting to discuss a capital expenditure. Your understanding of the analysis will allow you to explain with confidence why the investment should be made, or why it should not.

Internal Rate of Return Method

Calculating internal rate of return is similar to calculating net present value, but the variable is different. Rather than assuming a particular discount rate and then inspecting the present value of the investment, IRR calculates the actual return provided by the projected cash flows. That rate of return can then be compared with the company's hurdle rate to see if the investment passes the test.

In our example, the company is proposing to invest $3,000, and it will receive $1,300 in cash flow at the end of each of the following three years. You can't just use the gross total cash flow of $3,900 to figure the rate of return, because the return is spread out over three years. So we need to do some calculations.

First, here's another way of looking at IRR: it's the hurdle rate that makes net present value equal to zero. Remember, we said that as discount rates increase, NPV decreases? If you did NPV calculations using a higher and higher interest rate, you'd find NPV getting smaller and smaller until it finally turned negative, meaning the project no longer passed the hurdle rate. In the preceding example, if you tried 10 percent as the hurdle rate, you'd get an NPV of about $212. If you tried 20 percent, your NPV would be negative, at –$218. So the inflection point, where NPV equals zero, is somewhere between 10 percent and 20 percent. In theory, you could keep narrowing in until you found it. In practice, you can just use a financial calculator or a Web tool, and you will find that the point where NPV equals zero is 14.36 percent. That is the investment's internal rate of return.

IRR is an easy method to explain and present, because it allows for a quick comparison of the project's return to the hurdle rate. On the downside, it does not quantify the project's contribution to the overall value of the company, as NPV does. It also does not quantify the effects of an important variable, namely how long the company expects to enjoy the given rate of return. When competing projects have different durations, using IRR exclusively can lead you to favor a quick-payback project with a high-percentage return when you should be investing in longer-payback projects with lower-percentage returns. IRR also does not address the issue of *scale*. For example, an IRR of 20 percent does not tell you anything about the dollar size of the return. It could be 20 percent of $1 or 20 percent of $1 million. NPV, by contrast, does tell you the dollar amount. When the stakes are high, in short, it may make sense to use both IRR and NPV.

COMPARING THE THREE METHODS

We've been hinting at two lessons here. One is that the three methods we have reviewed may lead you to different decisions, depending on which one you rely on. The other is that the NPV method is the best choice when the methods conflict. Let's take another example and see how the differences play out.

Assume again that your company has $3,000 to invest. (Keeping the numbers small makes the calculations easier to follow.) It also has three different possible investments in different types of computer systems, as follows:

- *Investment A:* Returns cash flow of $1,000 per year for three years
- *Investment B:* Returns cash flow of $3,600 at the end of year one
- *Investment C:* Returns cash flow of $4,600 at the end of year three

The required rate of return—the hurdle rate—in your company is 9 percent, and all three investments carry similar levels of risk. If you could select only one of these investments, which would it be?

The payback method tells us how long it will take to get back the initial investment. Assuming the payback occurs at the end of each year, here is how it turns out:

- *Investment A:* Three years
- *Investment B:* One year
- *Investment C:* Three years

By this method alone, investment B is the clear winner. But if we run the calculations for net present value, here is how they turn out:

- *Investment A:* –$469 (negative!)
- *Investment B:* $303
- *Investment C:* $552

Now investment A is out, and investment C looks like the best choice. What does the internal rate of return method say?

- *Investment A:* 0 percent
- *Investment B:* 20 percent
- *Investment C:* 15.3 percent

Interesting. If we went by IRR alone, we would choose investment B. But the NPV calculation favors C—and that would be the correct decision. As NPV shows us, investment C is worth more in today's dollars than investment B.

The explanation? While B pays a higher return than C, it only pays that return for one year. With C we get a lower return, but we get it for three years. And three years at 15.3 percent is better than one year at 20 percent. Of course, if you assume you could keep on investing the money at 20 percent, then B would be better—but NPV can't take into account hypothetical future investments. What it does assume is that the company can go on earning 9 percent on its cash. Even so, if we take the $3,600 that investment B gives us at the end of year one and reinvest it at 9 percent, we still end up with less at the end of year three than we would get from investment C.

So it always makes sense to use NPV calculations for your investment decisions, even if you sometimes decide to use one of the other methods for discussion and presentation.

PROFITABILITY INDEX

The profitability index (PI) is a tool used to compare capital investments. Every company, after all, has limited capital. Most could invest that capital in a variety of different ways, and each investment would probably require a different amount of money. Calculating a PI helps you see which investments are likely to be most valuable to the business.

To calculate the PI, we first must perform NPV calculations for each investment. Then we take the *net* present value and add back the initial investment itself to get the present value. In our three examples, each required an initial investment of $3,000. Investment A had a net present value of –469 and a present value of $2,531. Investment B's NPV was $303, and its present value $3,303. For investment C the figures are $552 and $3,552, respectively. To convert these NPV results to a profitability index, just take the present value and *divide* by the initial investment. The calculations look like this:

- Investment A's PI is $2,531 divided by $3,000, or 0.84.
- Investment B's PI is $3,303 divided by $3,000, or 1.10.
- Investment C's PI is $3,552 divided by $3,000, or 1.18.

In other words, investment A pays $.84 in present dollars for every dollar invested. Investment B pays $1.10, and investment C pays $1.18. The index makes it possible to rank-order investments by their PI value—particularly useful when you are looking at opportunities requiring different levels of investment. One investment may carry a higher NPV than another, but if it costs more than the alternative, you don't have an accurate comparison. The PI solves this problem.

THE HARD PART

The key to useful ROI analysis—and the most difficult part of any method—is to make good estimates of the future benefits of an investment. It is where the real challenge lies and where the most common mistakes are made. Even big companies find this hard. Just look at the number of acquisitions or other major investments that don't pay off. These bad investments almost always reflect unrealistic projections of the project's future economic benefits.

How can you avoid making mistakes of this sort? The most important thing to remember is that your focus should be on cash flow, not on future profits. Maintaining this focus requires an additional analytic step when you are making projections, but the extra effort is worth it.

Let's consider an example—and since you're now more familiar with capital expenditure analysis, we'll use numbers more like those you would encounter in the real world (though still simplified). You have an opportunity to build a new plant that will increase your business's production capacity for three years. The plant costs $30 million and will last for four years (we'll continue to keep the time frames short for purposes of illustration). It will produce enough new product to generate $60 million in additional revenue in each of the next three years.

The projected incremental income statement for the project might look something like this:

	Year 1	Year 2	Year 3
Revenue	$60,000,000	$60,000,000	$60,000,000
Material and labor	30,000,000	30,000,000	30,000,000
Depreciation	10,000,000	10,000,000	10,000,000
Operating profit	20,000,000	20,000,000	20,000,000
Taxes	5,000,000	5,000,000	5,000,000
Net profit	$15,000,000	$15,000,000	$15,000,000

It looks like a good project, doesn't it? You invest $30 million and get a profit of $45 million over three years. But we have deliberately omitted a critical point. The example compares *profit* from the project to *cash* that was invested. As you'll remember from earlier chapters, profit is not the same as cash. Comparing a profit return to a cash investment is like comparing nectarines to bananas.

Typically, you need two steps to get from operating profit to cash. First you must add back any noncash expenses. Depreciation, for instance, is a noncash expense that lowers profit but does not affect cash flow. Second, you must consider the additional working capital. More sales will require more inventory and will lead to more accounts receivable—two key elements of working capital. Both of these investments will have to be financed with cash.

So let's assume that this new increase in sales will require you to sell to new customers that have poorer credit ratings than your current customers. Perhaps it will take sixty days to collect from these customers instead of forty-five days. Perhaps you will need to increase your accounts receivable by, say, $10 million during these three years. Meanwhile, assume that your inventory will need to increase by $5 million to cover the additional sales. (The finance people can estimate all these numbers with some precision on the basis of your past financials; for the purposes of this example, we're merely assuming what they will be.)

To convert the profit to cash flow, the calculation would look as follows:

	Year 1	Year 2	Year 3
Revenue	$60,000,000	$60,000,000	$60,000,000
Material and labor	30,000,000	30,000,000	30,000,000
Depreciation	10,000,000	10,000,000	10,000,000
Operating profit	20,000,000	20,000,000	20,000,000
Taxes	5,000,000	5,000,000	5,000,000
Net profit	$15,000,000	$15,000,000	$15,000,000
Add depreciation	10,000,000	10,000,000	10,000,000
Working capital	(15,000,000)	0	15,000,000
Net cash flow	$10,000,000	$25,000,000	$40,000,000

Now the project looks much more appealing. The calculations suggest that the $30 million investment will return $75 million over three years. Of course, you still need to apply net present value analysis to see if this investment makes sense for the business.

Remember the devil is in the details in ROI analysis. Anyone can make the projections look good enough so that the investment seems to make sense. Often it makes sense to do a *sensitivity analysis*—that is, check the calculations using future cash flows that are 80 percent or 90 percent of the original projections, and see if the investment still looks good. If it does, you can be more confident that your calculations are leading you to the right decision.

This chapter, we know, has involved a lot of calculating. But sometimes you'd be surprised at how intuitive the whole process can be. Not long ago, Joe was running a financial review meeting at Setpoint. A senior manager in the company was suggesting that Setpoint invest $80,000 in a new machining center so that it could produce certain parts in-house rather than relying on an outside vendor. Joe wasn't wild about the proposal for several reasons, but before he could speak up, a shop assembly technician asked the manager the following questions:

- Did you figure out the monthly cash flow return we will get on this new equipment? Eighty thousand dollars is a lot of money!
- Do you realize that we are in the spring, and the business is typically slow, and cash is tight during the summer?
- Have you figured in the cost of labor to run the machine? We are all pretty busy in the shop; you will probably have to hire someone to run this equipment.
- And are there better ways we could spend that cash to grow the business?

After this grilling, the manager dropped the proposal. The assembly technician might not have been an expert in net present value calculations, but he sure understood the concepts.

Intuition is great when it works. If you can make decisions (or challenge someone else's proposal) on gut feel, as the technician did, go ahead. With larger or more complex projects, however, intuition isn't sufficient; you need solid analysis as well. That's when you need the concepts and procedures outlined in this chapter.

Part Six
Toolbox

A STEP-BY-STEP GUIDE TO ANALYZING CAPITAL EXPENDITURES

You've been talking with your boss about buying a new piece of equipment for the plant, or maybe mounting a new marketing campaign. He ends the meeting abruptly. "Sounds good," he says. "Write me up a proposal with the ROI and have it on my desk by Monday."

Don't panic: here's a step-by-step guide to preparing your proposal.

1. Remember that ROI means return on investment—just another way of saying, "Prepare an analysis of this capital expenditure." The boss wants to know whether the investment is worth it, and he wants calculations to back it up.

2. Collect all the data you can about the cost of the investment. In the case of a new machine, total costs would include the purchase price, shipping costs, installation, factory downtime, debugging, training, and so on. Where you must make estimates, note that fact. Treat the total as your initial cash outlay. You will also need to determine the machine's useful life, not an easy task (but part of the art we enjoy so much!). You might talk to the manufacturer and to others who have purchased the equipment to help you answer the question.

3. Determine the benefits of the new investment, in terms of what it will save the company or what it will help the company earn. A calculation for a new machine should include any cost sav-

ings from greater output speed, less rework, a reduction in the number of people required to operate the equipment, increased sales because customers are happier, and so on. The tricky part here is that you need to figure out how all these factors translate into an estimate of cash flow, as we showed in chapter 27. Don't be afraid to ask for help from your finance department—they're trained in this kind of thing and should be willing to help.

4. Find out the company's hurdle rate for this kind of investment. Calculate the net present value of the project using this hurdle rate. Remember to use your finance department—they should have a spreadsheet that ensures you'll gather the data they believe is important and that you run the calculations the way they want them done.

5. Calculate payback and internal rate of return (the finance department's spreadsheet probably includes those as well). You'll probably get questions about what they are from your boss, so you need to have the answers ready.

6. Write up the proposal. Keep it brief. Describe the project, outline the costs and benefits (both financial and otherwise), and describe the risks. Discuss how it fits with the company's strategy or competitive situation. Then give your recommendations. Include your NPV, payback, and IRR calculations in case there are questions about how you arrived at your results.

Managers sometimes go overboard in writing up capital expenditure proposals. It's probably human nature: we all like new things, and it's usually pretty easy to make the numbers turn out so that the investment looks good. But we advise conservatism and caution. Explain exactly where you think the estimates are good and where you think they may be shaky. Do a sensitivity analysis, and show (if you can) that the estimate makes sense even if cash flows don't materialize at quite the level you hope. A conservative proposal is one that is likely to be funded—and one that is likely to add the most to the company's value in the long run.

One more comment. There are times when doing this kind of analysis isn't worth the time and trouble. Sometimes, for instance, a senior executive might ask you to justify a decision he has already made. There's really no point in doing the analysis (unless you can't get out of it). You will just have to fiddle with your assumptions and estimates until the numbers come out "right." We know of a small software company (less than $50 million in annual revenue) whose owner decided he wanted a corporate jet. He asked the company controller to do an ROI analysis on the jet to make sure it made economic sense. When the controller's numbers showed that the investment wasn't even in the ballpark for a business this size, the owner asked him to redo the analysis with "new" information. The numbers still did not justify the jet. Never mind: last we heard, the owner was just waiting to close a big sale and then planned to buy the jet anyway.

Then, too, some investments are "no brainers" and don't require detailed analysis. At Joe's company, Setpoint, engineers generate several hundred dollars a day in gross profit when they are working on a valuable project. If an engineer's CAD system goes down, he can't generate that profit. So let's imagine that Robert's computer is getting old and periodically crashes. If it's down for several days over the course of a year, the company might be forgoing thousands of dollars in gross profit. Meanwhile, a new computer costs $4,000. You don't need NPV or IRR to figure out that the new one is worth the money.

CALCULATING THE COST OF CAPITAL

How does a company determine the interest rate or discount rate to use when it does capital budgeting analysis? To answer this question you need to figure out the company's *cost of capital.*

Cost of capital can be a complex calculation. You'll need to know several things about the company, including:

- What is the proportion of debt and equity that it uses to finance its operations?
- How volatile is the company's stock?
- What is the overall interest cost on its debt?

- What are the prevailing interest rates in the market?
- What is the company's current tax rate?

Answering these questions allows you to determine the minimum return or interest rate required to justify an investment.

Let's look at an example. We'll assume that the answers to the questions are as follows:

- The company finances its operations with 30 percent debt and 70 percent equity. (You can derive these percentages from the balance sheet.)
- The stock's volatility, as measured by its beta, is 1.25. (*Beta* measures the volatility of a security compared with the market as a whole. Stocks that typically rise and fall with the market, like those of many large industrial companies, have a beta close to 1.0. More volatile companies, which tend to rise and fall more than the market, might have a beta of 2.0, and companies that are stable relative to the market, such as utilities, might have betas of 0.65. The higher the beta, the riskier the stock in the eyes of investors.)
- The average interest rate on the company's debt is 6 percent.
- The interest rate on a risk-free US treasury bill is 3 percent; a typical investment in the stock market is expected to provide an 11 percent return.
- The company's tax rate is 25 percent.

Armed with this information, we can determine the company's *weighted average cost of capital* (WACC)—that is, the cost of its debt and equity weighted by the 70-to-30 percent ratio. The WACC is the minimum return that a company must earn on its asset base to satisfy creditors, owners, and everyone else who provides capital.

The first step is to calculate the cost of debt. Since the interest on debt is deductible for taxes, we need to look at both the interest rate and the tax rate to determine the after-tax cost. Here's the formula:

$$\text{Cost of debt} = \text{average interest cost of debt} \times (1 - \text{tax rate})$$

So for our business this would be:

$$\text{Cost of debt} = 6\% \times (1.00 - .25) = 4.5\%$$

The next step is to calculate the cost of the company's equity by using beta (risk) and prevailing interest rates. Here's the equation:

$$\text{Cost of equity} = \text{risk-free interest rate} + \text{beta} \times (\text{market rate} - \text{risk free rate})$$

In the example, it is as follows:

$$\text{Cost of equity} = 3\% + 1.25 \times (11\% - 3\%) = 13\%$$

The analysis shows that this company has an after-tax cost of debt of 4.5 percent and a cost of equity of 13 percent.

Finally, we know that the company is 30 percent debt and 70 percent equity. So the weighted average cost of capital (WACC) would be:

$$(0.3 \times 4.5\%) + (0.7 \times 13) = 10.45\%$$

The minimum return the business should get on its investments is 10.45 percent. That's a return that justifies its use of capital.

As you look at the numbers, you might ask, "Why not use more low-cost debt and less high-cost equity? Wouldn't that lower the business's cost of capital?" It might—but it also might not. Taking on more debt increases risk. This perceived risk might increase the beta of the stock and thus raise the cost of equity still further. Extra risk might also persuade debtholders to demand a higher return. These increases might wipe out the gain from increasing debt.

A business's finance group must determine the right mix of debt to equity to minimize its WACC. This mix is tough to get exactly right, and it changes as interest rates and perceived risks change. If the finance folks do get it right, they're certainly earning their keep.

WACC is often considered the minimum return a business should earn on its capital investments. Most large companies evaluate their WACC annually and use it as a benchmark to set the hurdle rate for NPV and other capital budgeting calculations. In actually determining the hurdle rate, however, companies often add two or three percentage points to the WACC, just for a margin of error.

ECONOMIC VALUE ADDED AND ECONOMIC PROFIT—PUTTING IT ALL TOGETHER

Economic value added (EVA) and economic profit (EP) are widely used measures for assessing a firm's financial performance. They measure much the same thing, but they are calculated slightly differently.

Economic value added, as far as we know, is the only measure that is actually a registered trademark of a consulting firm. (It is owned by the New York firm Stern Stewart & Co.) The underlying idea is this: a company adds value for its shareholders only if it earns a risk-adjusted profit greater than what it could have earned by investing that same capital elsewhere.

To calculate EVA and EP, you begin by calculating return on total capital (ROTC). Then you subtract the WACC. Proponents of the two measures point out that a company must incur costs to purchase the operating assets that it uses to generate profits, whether it uses equity or debt or some combination. To understand a company's true profit, you ought to take those costs into account.

We'll look at the same example we used in the previous entry and see how that company is doing by these measures. Remember that this company's WACC was 10.45 percent. We'll also say that its ROTC was 9.6 percent, just as in the example in chapter 21. Now here's the formula for EVA:

$$\text{EVA} = \text{ROTC} - \text{WACC}$$

So for our business, it is:

$$\text{EVA} = 9.60\% - 10.45\% = -0.85\%$$

In short, the EVA for this company is negative. It earned a return for the capital providers that was nearly 1 percentage point lower than what they would typically expect. If the EVA for this business continues to be negative, shareholders and lenders will be likely to look elsewhere.

Now let's look at what this negative EVA means for economic profit. EP converts the EVA percentage to a dollar amount; you just multiply EVA by total capital, calculated as we showed you in chapter 21. So if the total capital invested in the business is $3.646 billion as in the example in chapter 21, the calculation looks like this:

$$EP = -0.85 \times \$3.646 \text{ billion or } -\$30{,}991{,}000$$

The capital providers are $31 million behind what they could reasonably expect from this business as a return.

What about the next year? Suppose that the company's performance improves, and it achieves an ROTC of 12 percent. Its WACC, meanwhile, drops to 9.5 percent due to decreases in interest rates. The only thing that remains the same is total capital. Now its EVA is 12% – 9.5% or 2.5%, and its EP is 2.5% × $3.646 billion, or $91,150,000. That's quite an improvement, and the providers of capital are no doubt happy.

Part Seven

Applied Financial Intelligence: Working Capital Management

28

The Magic of Managing the Balance Sheet

WE'VE MENTIONED THE PHRASE *managing the balance sheet* a couple of times in this book. Right now we want to go into greater detail about how to do it. The reason? Astute management of the balance sheet is like financial magic. It allows a company to improve its financial performance even without boosting sales or lowering costs. Better balance sheet management makes a business more efficient at converting inputs to outputs and ultimately to cash. It speeds up the *cash conversion cycle*, a concept that we'll take up later in this part. Companies that can generate more cash in less time have greater freedom of action; they aren't so dependent on outside investors or lenders.

To be sure, the finance organization in your company is ultimately responsible for managing most of the balance sheet. They're the ones responsible for figuring out how much to borrow and on what terms, for lining up equity investment when necessary, and for generally keeping an eye on the company's overall assets and liabilities. But nonfinancial managers have a huge impact on certain key line items from the balance sheet, which taken together are known as *working capital*. Working capital is a prime arena for the development and application of financial intelligence. Once you grasp the concept, you'll become a valuable partner to the finance organization and senior managers. Learn to manage working capital better, and you can have a powerful effect on both your company's profitability and its cash position.

THE ELEMENTS OF WORKING CAPITAL

Working capital is a category of resources that includes cash, inventory, and receivables, minus whatever a company owes in the short term. It comes straight from the balance sheet, and it's often calculated according to the following formula:

working capital = current assets – current liabilities

Of course, this equation can be broken down further. Current assets, as we have seen, includes items such as cash, receivables, and inventory. Current liabilities includes payables and other short-term obligations. But these aren't isolated balance sheet line items; they represent different stages of the production cycle and different forms of working capital.

To understand this, imagine a small manufacturing company. Every production cycle begins with cash, which is the first component of working capital. The company takes the cash and buys some raw materials. That creates raw-materials inventory, a second component of working capital. Then the raw materials are used in production, creating work-in-process inventory and eventually finished-goods inventory, also part of the "inventory" component of working capital. Finally, the company sells the goods to customers, creating receivables, which are the third and last component of working capital (figure 28-1). In a service business, the cycle is similar but simpler. For example, our own company—the Business Literacy Institute—is primarily a training business. Its operating cycle involves the time required to go from the initial development of training materials to

Working Capital

Working capital is the money a company needs to finance its daily operations. Accountants usually measure it by adding up a company's cash, inventory, and accounts receivable, and then subtracting short-term debts.

FIGURE 28-1

Working capital and the production cycle

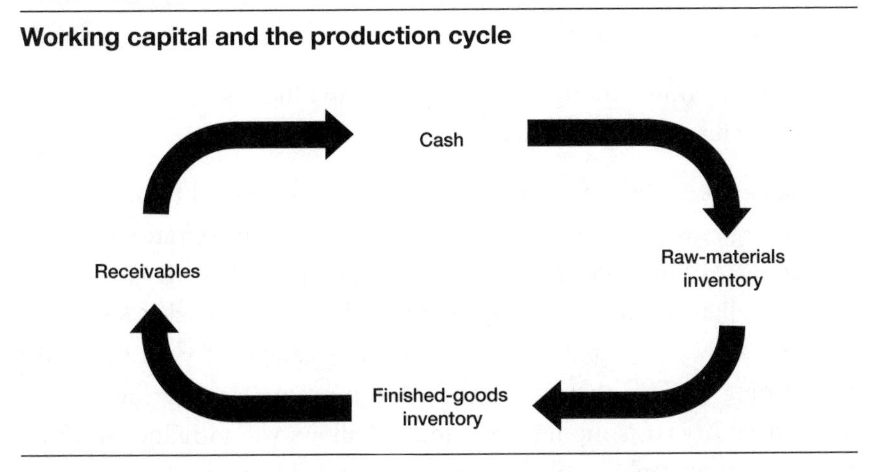

completion of training classes and finally to collection of the bill. The more efficient we are in finishing a project and following up on collections, the healthier our profitability and cash flow will be. In fact, the best way to make money in a service business is to provide the service quickly and well, then collect as soon as possible.

Throughout this cycle, the *form* taken by working capital changes. But the *amount* doesn't change unless more cash enters the system—for example, from loans or from equity investments.

Of course, if the company buys on credit, then some of the cash remains intact—but a corresponding "payables" line is created on the liabilities side of the balance sheet. So that must be deducted from the three other components to get an accurate picture of the company's working capital.

MEASURING WORKING CAPITAL

Companies generally look at three main components when measuring working capital: accounts receivable, inventory, and accounts payable. A change in any of these elements either increases or decreases working capital, as follows:

- *Accounts receivable* is the use of cash to finance customers' purchases, so an increase in A/R increases working capital.

- *Inventory* is the use of cash to purchase and stock inventory for sale to customers, so an increase in inventory also increases working capital.
- *Accounts payable*, though, is money owed to others, so an increase in A/P decreases working capital.

You can use a few of the ratios we've already discussed to understand and manage working capital. As you might imagine, these ratios all measure either A/R, inventory, or A/P. Days sales outstanding (DSO), as you might recall, measures the average time it takes to collect sales. So reducing DSO allows a company to reduce working capital. Days in inventory outstanding (DII) is the number of days inventory stays in the system. Since inventory costs money, reducing DII allows you to reduce working capital. By now you've probably guessed the third key measure: days payable outstanding, or DPO. If you increase DPO—take longer to pay your bills—you reduce working capital. We'll discuss managing these elements of working capital in chapters 29 and 30.

Overall, how much working capital is appropriate for a company? This question doesn't allow an easy answer. Every company needs enough cash and inventory to do its job. The larger it is and the faster it is growing, the more working capital it is likely to need. But the real challenge is to use working capital efficiently. The three working capital accounts that nonfinancial managers can truly affect are accounts receivable, inventory, and (to a lesser extent) accounts payable. We'll take up each one in turn.

Before we do, though, it's worth asking once again how much "art" is involved in all these calculations. In this case, the best answer might be "some." Cash is a hard number, not easily subject to manipulation. Receivables and payables are relatively hard as well. Inventory isn't quite so hard. Various accounting techniques and assumptions allow a company to value inventory in different ways. So a company's calculation of working capital will depend to an extent on the rules the company follows. Still, you can generally assume that working capital figures aren't subject to as much discretion and judgment as many of the numbers we learned about earlier.

29

Your Balance Sheet Levers

MOST COMPANIES USE THEIR CASH to finance customers' purchase of products or services. That's the "accounts receivable" line on the balance sheet—the amount of money customers owe at a given point in time, based on the value of what they have purchased before that date.

The key ratio that measures accounts receivable, as we saw in part 5, is days sales outstanding, or DSO—that is, the average number of days it takes to collect on these receivables. *The longer a company's DSO, the more working capital is required to run the business.* Customers have more of its cash in the form of products or services not yet paid for, so that cash isn't available to buy inventory, deliver more services, and so on. Conversely, the shorter a company's DSO, the less working capital is required to run the business. It follows that the more people who understand DSO and work to bring it down, the more free cash the company will have at its disposal.

MANAGING DSO

The first step in managing DSO is to understand what it is and in which direction it has been heading. If it's higher than it ought to be, and particularly if it's trending upward (which it nearly always seems to be), managers need to begin asking questions.

Operations and *R&D* managers, for example, must ask themselves whether there are any problems with the products that might make customers less willing to pay their bills. Is the company selling what customers want and expect? Is there a problem with delivery? Quality problems and late deliveries often provoke late payment, just because customers are not pleased with the products they're receiving and decide that they will take their own sweet time about payment. Managers in quality assurance, market research, product development, and so on thus have an effect on receivables, as do managers in production and shipping. In a service company, people who are out delivering the service need to ask themselves the same questions. If service customers aren't satisfied with what they're getting, they too will take their time about paying.

Customer-facing managers—those in sales and customer service—have to ask a similar set of questions. Are our customers healthy? What is the standard in their industry for paying bills? Are they in a region of the world that pays fast or slow? Salespeople typically have the first contact with a customer, so it is up to them to flag any concerns about the customer's financial health. Once the sale is made, customer-service reps need to pick up the ball and learn what's going on. What's happening at the customer's shop? Are they working overtime? Laying people off? Meanwhile, salespeople need to work with the folks in credit and customer service so that everybody understands the terms up front and will notice when a customer is late. At one company we worked with, the delivery people knew the most about customers' situations because they were at their facilities every day. They would alert sales and accounting if there seemed to be issues cropping up in a customer's business.

Credit managers need to ask whether the terms offered are good for the company and whether they fit the credit histories of the customers. They need to make judgments about whether the company is giving credit too easily or whether it is too tough in its credit policies. There's always a tradeoff between increasing sales on the one hand and issuing credit to poorer credit risks on the other. Credit managers need to set the precise terms they're willing to offer. Is net thirty days satisfactory—or should we allow net sixty? They need to determine strategies such as offering discounts for early pay. For example, "2/10 net 30" means that customers get a discount of 2 percent if they pay their bill in ten days and no discount if they wait thirty days. Sometimes a 1 or 2 percent discount can help a struggling company collect its receivables and thereby lower its DSO—but of course it does so by eating into profitability.

We know of a small company that has a simple, homegrown approach to the issue of giving credit to customers. The company has identified the traits it wants in its customers, and has even named its ideal customer "Bob." Bob's qualities include the following:

- He works for a large company.
- His company is known for paying its bills on time.
- He can maintain and understand the product provided (this company makes complex, technology-intensive products).
- He is looking for an ongoing relationship.

If a new customer meets these criteria, his company will get credit from this small manufacturer. Otherwise it won't. As a result of this policy, the company has been able to keep its DSO quite low and to grow without additional equity investment.

All these decisions greatly affect accounts receivable and thus working capital. And the fact is, they can have a huge impact. Reducing DSO even by one day can save a large company millions of dollars per day. For example, check back to the DSO calculation in chapter 24, and you'll note that one day of sales in our sample company is just over $24 million. Reducing DSO from fifty-five days to fifty-four in this company would thus increase cash by $24 million. That's cash that can be used for other things in the business.

MANAGING INVENTORY

Many managers (and consultants!) these days are focusing on inventory. They work to reduce inventory wherever possible. They use buzzwords such as *lean manufacturing*, *just-in-time inventory management*, and *economic order quantity* (EOQ). The reason for all this attention is exactly what we're talking about here. Managing inventory efficiently reduces working capital requirements by freeing up large amounts of cash.

The challenge for inventory management, of course, isn't to reduce inventory to zero, which would probably leave a lot of customers unsatisfied. The challenge is to reduce it to a minimum level while still ensuring that every raw material and every part will be available when needed and every product will be ready for sale when a customer wants it. A manufacturer needs to be constantly ordering raw material, making things, and holding them for delivery to customers. Wholesalers and retailers need to replenish their stocks regularly, and avoid the dreaded "stockout"—an item that isn't available when a customer wants it. Yet every item in inventory ties up cash, which means that the cash cannot be used for other purposes. Exactly how much inventory is required to satisfy customers while minimizing that tied-up cash, well, that's the million-dollar question (and the reason for all those consultants).

The techniques for managing inventory are beyond the scope of this book. But we do want to emphasize that many different kinds of managers affect a company's use of inventory—which means that all these managers can have an impact on reducing working capital requirements. For example:

- *Salespeople* love to tell customers they can have exactly what they want. ("Have it *your* way," as the old Burger King jingle put it.) Custom paint job? No problem. Bells and whistles? No problem. But every variation requires a little more inventory, meaning a little more cash. Obviously, customers must be satisfied. But that commonsense requirement has to be balanced against the fact that inventory costs money. The more that salespeople can sell standard products with limited variations, the less inventory their company will have to carry.

- *Engineers* love those same bells and whistles. In fact, they're constantly working to improve the company's products, replacing version 2.54 with version 2.55, and so on. Again, this is a laudable business objective, but one that has to be balanced against inventory requirements. A proliferation of product versions puts a burden on inventory management. When a product line is kept simple, with a few easily interchangeable options, inventory declines and inventory management becomes a less taxing task.

- *Production departments* greatly affect inventory. For instance, what's the percentage of machine downtime? Frequent breakdowns require the company to carry more work-in-process inventory and more finished-goods inventory. And what's the average time between changeovers? Decisions about how much to build of a particular part have an enormous impact on inventory requirements. Even the layout of a plant affects inventory: an efficiently designed production flow in an efficient plant minimizes the need for inventory.

Along these lines, it's worth noting that many US plants operate on a principle that eats up tremendous amounts of working capital. When business is slow, they nevertheless keep on churning out product in order to maintain factory efficiency. Plant managers focus on keeping unit costs down, often because that goal has been pounded into their heads for so long that they no longer question it. They have been trained to do it, told to do it, and paid (with bonuses) for achieving it.

When business is good, the goal makes perfect sense: keeping unit costs down is simply a way of managing all the costs of production in an efficient manner. (This is the old approach of focusing only on the income statement, which is fine as far as it goes.) When demand is slow, however, the plant manager must consider the company's cash as well as its unit costs. A plant that continues to turn out product in these circumstances is just creating more inventory that will sit on a shelf taking up space. Coming to work and reading a book might be better than building product that is not ready to be sold.

How much can a company save through astute inventory management? Look again at our sample company: cutting *just one day* out of the DII number—reducing it from seventy-four days to seventy-three—would increase cash by nearly $19 million. Any large company can save millions of dollars of cash, and thereby reduce working capital requirements—just by making modest improvements in its inventory management.

30

Homing In on Cash Conversion

IN THIS CHAPTER WE'LL TAKE UP THE CASH CONVERSION CYCLE, which measures how effective a company is at collecting its cash. But there's one little wrinkle we have to consider first—how fast a company decides to pay the money it owes its vendors.

Accounts payable is a tough number to get right. It's an area where finance meets philosophy. Financial considerations alone would encourage managers to maximize days payable outstanding (DPO), thus conserving the company's cash. A change in this ratio is as powerful as a change in the other ratios we've been discussing. In our sample company, for instance, increasing DPO by just one day would add about $19 million to the company's cash balance.

Companies do often use DPO as a tool to increase cash flow and reduce the amount of working capital tied up in the business. During the financial crisis that began in 2008 and the subsequent recession, for instance, many corporations increased their DPO as a strategy to conserve cash. In fact, one *Fortune* 50 company actually told suppliers it would pay them in 120 days.

But is this a good strategy for ordinary times? Or for companies that are not part of the *Fortune* 50? The strategy carries residual costs that are hard to assess. Sure, the finance team can measure how much cash is generated by increasing DPO from sixty days to seventy. For a large company, that can be a significant amount. But what about the "soft" costs? A company that delays payments may put a key supplier out of business. It may find that suppliers are raising their prices to cover the cost of the additional financing they must line up. It may face slower delivery times and even lower quality—after all, the suppliers are likely to feel squeezed and will have to cope as best they can. Some suppliers may even decline the company's business. Another practical consideration is the company's Dun & Bradstreet rating. D&B bases its scores, in part, on a company's payment history. An organization that consistently pays late may find that it has trouble later on getting a loan.

A personal story illustrates the point. In the early days of Joe's manufacturing company, Setpoint, the company's founders told him that "net 30" meant just that: net 30. Setpoint would always pay its suppliers in thirty days. The founders had previously worked for a struggling company that routinely delayed its payables to one hundred days or more. As engineers, they were often unable to get parts for critical projects until the suppliers were paid. That delayed the projects and thus delayed revenue payments based on project completion, creating a downward spiral. Because of their experience, Setpoint's founders decided never to be in that position with their own business.

The policy created a problem for Joe, because Setpoint's primary customer at the time, a large corporation, paid in forty-five to sixty days. So Joe took one of the founders to the bank to discuss a credit line. He showed the banker how much cash they were likely to need. The banker responded, "I don't know why you need this line. Just delay paying your suppliers by twenty days and you will be fine."

The founder spoke firmly but quietly. "If I delay paying my suppliers, are they going to provide me with quality product on time? I need suppliers I can trust. That's what the business depends on. If I delay paying them by twenty days, what will that do to my relationship with them?"

The young banker just stared. Finally he agreed to look into a credit line for Setpoint. Setpoint eventually got the line, and for nearly twenty years, with few exceptions, has stayed at net 30 with its suppliers. The policy has cost the company money because it raises working capital requirements. But while it puts constraints on cash flow, Setpoint's leaders believe that it positively affects the company's reputation and relationship with its vendors—and in the long term helps to build a stronger community of businesses around the company.

We won't go into any more detail about payables policies, because in most companies nonfinancial managers don't have much direct impact on how fast the company pays its bills. But in general, if you notice that your company's DPO is climbing—and particularly if it is higher than your DSO—you might want to ask the finance folks a few questions. After all, your work probably depends on good relationships with vendors, and—like Setpoint's founders—you don't want finance to mess up those relationships unnecessarily.

THE CASH CONVERSION CYCLE

Another way to understand working capital is to study the *cash conversion cycle*. It's essentially a timeline relating the stages of production (the operating cycle) to the company's investment in working capital. The timeline has three levels, and you can see how the levels are linked in figure 30-1. Understanding these three levels and their measures provides a powerful way of understanding the business. It should help you make good decisions.

Starting at the left, the company purchases raw materials. That begins the accounts payable period and the inventory period. In the next phase, the company has to pay for those raw materials. That begins the cash conversion cycle itself—the cash has now been paid out, and the job is to see how fast it can come back. Yet the company is still in its inventory period; it hasn't actually sold any finished goods yet.

Eventually, the company does sell its finished goods, ending the inventory period. But it is just entering the accounts receivable period; it still hasn't received any cash. Finally, it does collect the cash on its sales, which ends both the accounts receivable period and the cash conversion cycle.

Why is all of this important? Because we can use it to determine how many days all this takes and then understand how many days a company's cash is tied up. That's an important number for managers and leaders to know. Armed with the information, managers can potentially find ways

FIGURE 30-1

The cash conversion cycle

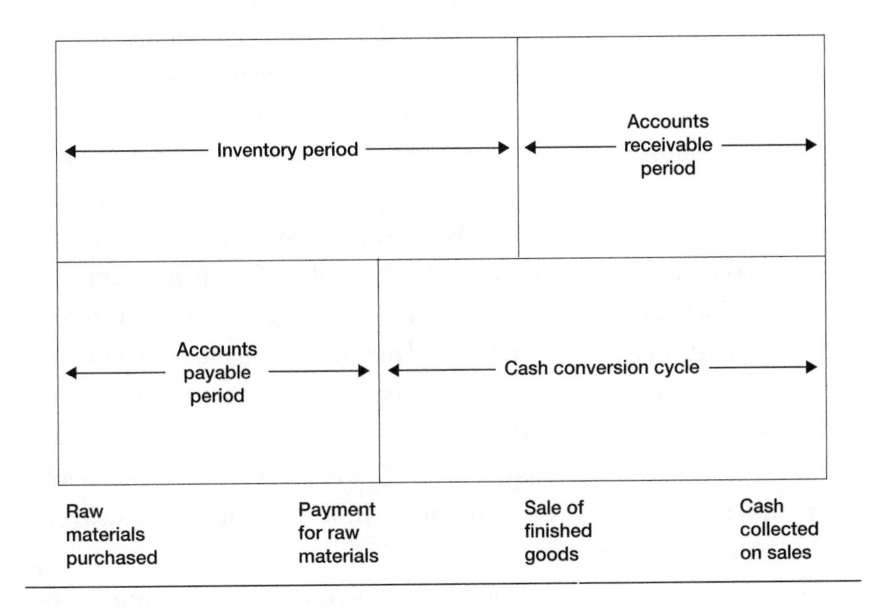

to "save" lots of cash for their company. To figure it out, use the following formula:

$$\text{cash conversion cycle} = \text{DSO} + \text{DII} - \text{DPO}$$

In other words, take days sales outstanding, add days in inventory, and subtract the number of days payable outstanding. That tells you, in days, how fast the company recovers its cash, from the moment it pays its payables to the moment it collects its receivables.

The cash conversion cycle gives you a way of calculating how much cash it takes to finance the business: you just take sales per day and multiply it by the number of days in the cash conversion cycle. Here are the calculations for our sample company:

DSO	+	DII	–	DPO	=	cash conversion cycle
54 days	+	74 days	–	55 days	=	73 days
73 days	×	$24,136,000 sales/day			=	$1,761,928,000

This business requires working capital of around $1.8 billion just to finance its operations. That isn't unusual for a large corporation. Even small companies require a lot of working capital relative to their sales if their cash conversion cycle is as long as sixty days. Companies of any size can get themselves into trouble on this score. Tyco International—mentioned earlier in this book—was famous for acquiring six hundred companies in two years. All those acquisitions entailed a lot of challenges, but one serious one involved huge increases in the cash conversion cycle. The reason? Tyco often was acquiring companies in the same industry, and competing products were added to its product list. Now that Tyco had several very similar products in inventory, the inventory didn't move as fast as it once had—and inventory days began to spiral out of control, increasing in some parts of the business by more than ten days. In a multinational company with more than $30 billion in revenue, increases on that scale can deplete cash by several hundred million dollars! (This is an issue that Tyco has long since addressed by closing down the acquisition pipeline and focusing on the operations of the business.)

The cash conversion cycle can be shortened by all the techniques discussed in this part: decreasing DSO, decreasing inventory, and increasing DPO. Find out what your company's cycle is and which direction it's heading in. You may want to discuss it with the folks in finance. Who knows? They might even be impressed that you know what it is and what levers can affect it. More important, you might start a conversation that will result in a faster cash conversion cycle, lower working capital requirements, and more free cash. That will benefit everybody in the business.

Part Seven
Toolbox

ACCOUNTS RECEIVABLE AGING

Want to manage accounts receivable more effectively? DSO is not the only measure to look at. Another is what's called the *aging* of receivables. Often, reviewing aging is the key to understanding the true situation in your company's receivables.

Here's why. As we mentioned earlier, DSO is by definition an average. For example, if you have $1 million in receivables that are under ten days and $1 million that are more than ninety days, your overall DSO is about fifty days. That doesn't sound too bad—but in fact, your company may be in substantial trouble, because half of its customers don't seem to be paying their bills. Another business of the same size might have a DSO figure of fifty days with only $250,000 over ninety days. That business isn't in the same sort of trouble.

An aging analysis will present you with just these kinds of figures: total receivables under thirty days, total for thirty to sixty days, and so on. It's usually worth checking out that analysis as well as your overall DSO number to get the full picture of your receivables.

Part Eight

Creating a Financially Intelligent Company

31

Financial Literacy and Corporate Performance

WE HAVE WRITTEN THIS BOOK IN HOPES of increasing your financial intelligence and helping you become a better leader, manager, or employee. We firmly believe that understanding the financial statements, the ratios, and everything else we have included in the book will make you more effective on the job and will better your career prospects. We also think that understanding the financial side of the business will make your work life more meaningful. You would never play baseball or backgammon without first learning how the game is played; why should business be any different? Knowing the rules—how profits are figured, why return on assets matters to shareholders, and all the rest—lets you see your work in the big-picture context of business enterprise, which is simply people working together to achieve certain objectives. You'll see more clearly how the company that you're a part of operates. You'll want to contribute to it, and you'll know how to do so. You'll be able to assess your performance better than you could before, because you can see which way the key numbers are moving and understand *why* they're moving in one direction or the other.

Then, of course, there's the fun of it. As we've shown, the financial report cards of business are partly reflections of reality. But they're also—sometimes very much so—reflections of estimates, assumptions, educated guesswork, and all the resulting biases. (Occasionally they reflect outright manipulation as well.) The folks in your company's finance organization know all this, but many of them haven't done a good job of sharing their knowledge with the rest of us. Now you get to ask them the tough questions. How do they recognize a particular category of revenue? Why did they choose a particular time frame for depreciation? Why is DII on the upswing? Of course, once they get past the shock of hearing that nonfinancial colleagues speak their language, they'll almost certainly be willing to discuss the bases for their assumptions and estimates, and modify them when appropriate. Who knows? They may even start asking for your advice.

BETTER COMPANIES

We also believe that businesses perform better when the financial intelligence quotient is higher. A healthy business, after all, is a good thing. It offers valuable goods and services to its customers. It provides its employees with stable jobs, pay raises, and opportunities for advancement. It pays a good return to its shareholders. Overall, healthy businesses help our economy grow, keep our communities strong, and improve our standard of living.

Financially intelligent managers contribute to a business's health because they can make better decisions. They can use their knowledge to help the company succeed. They manage resources more wisely and use financial information more astutely, and thereby increase their company's profitability and cash flow. They also understand more about *why* things happen, and can lend a shoulder to the wheel instead of just carping about how misguided the senior leadership is. We remember, for example, teaching a class of sales executives, using their company's actual financials. When we got to the cash flow statement—and showed them how the company's cash coffers had been drained to pursue growth by acquisition—one of the sales executives smiled. We asked him why he was smiling, and he laughed. "I've been fighting with the vice president of sales in my division for the better part of a year," he said. "The reason is, they changed our commission plan. We used to be paid on sales, and now we're paid when the sales are collected. Finally I understand the reason for the change." He went on to explain that he agreed with the strategy of growth by acquisition, and he really didn't mind that the comp plan had been changed to support the strategy. But he had never understood *why*.

Financial intelligence makes for healthier business in another sense, too. A lot of companies today are governed by politics and power. They reward people who curry favor with their superiors and who build behind-the-scenes alliances. Gossip and mistrust are rife; common objectives get lost as individuals scurry to ensure their own advancement. At its worst, this kind of environment becomes truly toxic. At one company we worked with, employees thought that profit-sharing bonuses were distributed only in years when employees complained loudly enough that they were unhappy. The purpose of profit sharing, they figured, was to keep them quiet. In reality, the company had a fairly straightforward plan that linked employees' efforts to their quarterly profit-sharing checks. But the politics were such that employees never believed the plan was real.

There's a simple antidote to politics: sunlight, transparency, and open communication. When people understand a company's objectives and work to attain them, it's easier to create an organization built on a sense of trust and a feeling of community. *In the long run, that kind of organization will always be more successful than its less open counterparts.* Sure, an Enron or a WorldCom or a Lehman Brothers can prosper for a while under secretive, self-serving leadership. But an organization that is successful over the long haul will almost invariably be built around trust, communication, and a shared sense of purpose. Financial training—an increase in financial intelligence—can make a big difference. At the company where employees thought that the purpose of profit sharing was to keep them quiet, those who underwent training learned how the plan really worked. Soon they were focusing their efforts on the numbers they affected—and soon they were getting a profit-sharing check every quarter.

Finally, financially savvy managers can react more quickly to the unexpected. There's a famous book called *Warfighting*, prepared by staff members of the US Marine Corps, that was first published in 1989 and since then has become a kind of bible for special forces of all kinds.[1] One theme of the book is that marines in combat are always faced with uncertainty and rapidly changing conditions. They can rarely rely on instructions from above; instead they must make decisions on their own. So it's imperative that commanders spell out their broad objectives and then leave decisions about implementation to junior officers and ordinary marines in the field. That's a lesson that's just as valuable to companies in today's mercurial business climate. Managers have to make a lot of day-to-day decisions without consulting the higher-ups. If they understand the financial parameters they're working under, those decisions can be made more quickly and effectively. The company's performance—like the performance of a marine unit on the ground—will be that much stronger.

TAKING IT TO THE TROOPS

There's a next step here as well. If it makes a difference for managers to understand finance, imagine how much more of a difference it would make if everybody in a department—indeed, everybody in a company—understood it.

The same logic applies: people in offices, in stores and warehouses, on shop floors, and at client sites can make smarter decisions if they know something about how their unit is measured and about the financial implications of what they do every day. Should they rework a damaged part or use a new one? Should they work fast to get as much done as possible or work more deliberately to ensure fewer mistakes? Should they spend their time developing new services or cultivating and serving existing customers? How important is it to have everything a customer might possibly need? Like marines, frontline employees and supervisors should know the broad outlines of what the organization needs so that they can work smarter on the job.

Companies understand this idea, of course, and in recent years have deluged employees and supervisors with performance goals, key performance indicators (KPIs), and other metrics. Maybe you have been the one to inform people of the KPIs they'll be evaluated on; if so, you know that there's typically a good deal of eye rolling and head shaking, particularly if the KPIs this quarter are different from last quarter's. But what if the folks in the field understood the financial logic of the KPIs or the performance goals? What if they understood that they are facing new KPIs this quarter not because some executive randomly decided it but because the company's financial situation had changed? Like the sales executive in the class, most people are willing to adapt to a new situation, *provided* they understand the reason for the change. If they don't understand, they'll wonder if management really knows what it's doing.

Just as financial intelligence in the managerial ranks can boost a business's performance, so can financial intelligence among the troops. The Center for Effective Organizations, for instance, conducted a study that looked at (among other things) many measures of employee involvement.[2] Two measures in particular were "sharing information about business performance, plans and goals" and training employees in "skills in understanding the business." Both of these were positively related to productivity, customer satisfaction, quality, speed, profitability, competitiveness, and employee satisfaction. The more that organizations trained their people in financial literacy, in other words, the better the organizations did. Other students of management, including Daniel R. Denison, Peter Drucker, and Jeffrey Pfeffer, have studied and supported the idea that the more employees understand the business, the better the business performs. All these findings should come as no surprise. When people understand what's going on, the level of trust in the organization rises. Turnover drops. Motivation and commitment increase. Does anybody doubt that greater trust, motivation, and commitment lead to better performance?

One of us, Joe, has seen all these phenomena firsthand. He and his partners have spent years building a business, Setpoint, from the ground up. Like every start-up, it experienced periodic difficulties and crises, and more than once the company's accountant told Joe that it couldn't survive another period of turbulence. But somehow it always did. Finally, the accountant confessed to Joe, "You know, I think the reason why you get through these difficult times is because you train your employees and share the finances with them. When times are tough, the company rallies together and finds a way to fight through it."

The accountant was right: the employees all do know exactly where the company stands. Sharing financial information and helping subordinates and coworkers to understand it is a way of creating a common purpose in a company. It fosters an environment where teamwork can survive and prosper. What's more, it's pretty tough for anyone to cook the books when they're open for everybody to see.

Of course, sharing the financials isn't enough. People have to understand them, and that usually requires training. This may be why more and more companies are now including financial intelligence training as part of their educational offerings. Some of the training programs are required; some are voluntary. All focus on the idea that if employees, managers, and leaders understand how financial success is measured, the company is going to be more successful. There are plenty of ways to increase financial intelligence, whether for a team, a department, a division, or a whole company. Our organization, the Business Literacy Institute, has taught not only leadership and management teams but also salespeople, human resources and IT personnel, operations people, engineers, project managers, and others about the financial side of their business. The following chapter will give you some specific ideas about how to increase the level of financial intelligence in your organization.

32

Financial Literacy Strategies

IF YOUR GOAL IS TO HAVE A financially intelligent workplace or department, your first step is to figure out a strategy for getting there. We don't use the word *strategy* lightly. You can't just sponsor a one-time training course or hand out an instruction book and expect everyone to be enlightened. People need to be engaged in the learning. The material needs to be repeated, then revisited in different ways. Financial literacy needs to become part of a company's culture. That takes time, effort, and even a little monetary investment.

But it's very doable. In this chapter, we'll offer some suggestions for both smaller companies and larger ones. You don't need to limit yourself to just one category or the other, however. All the suggestions work in both contexts; the differences are often a matter of logistics and budgets. Large companies, for instance, are accustomed to producing formal training programs, while smaller companies may need to improvise. And a small company may not have much money to spend on training—although we believe that this is one of the few training programs that has a direct impact on the bottom line.

SMALL-COMPANY TOOLS AND TECHNIQUES

The following tools and techniques hardly constitute an exhaustive list. But they are all approaches that any manager or company owner can implement fairly easily on his or her own initiative.

Training (Over and Over)

Start by putting together three short, informal training sessions. We don't mean anything fancy: even a PowerPoint presentation with some handouts works fine (though we would caution you that PowerPoint isn't always conducive to lasting learning!). Each session should last between thirty and sixty minutes. Focus on one financial concept per session. Joe, for example, conducts three one-hour courses at Setpoint—on the income statement, on cash flow and project finance, and on the balance sheet. Depending on your situation, you might look at gross margin, selling expenses as a percent of sales, or even inventory turns. The concept should be relevant to your team's job, and you should show people how they affect the numbers.

Offer these classes on a *regular* basis, maybe once a month. Let people attend two or three times if they want—it often takes that long for folks to get it. Encourage 100 percent attendance among your direct reports. Create an environment that tells the participants you believe they are an important part of the success of the company and that you want their involvement. Eventually, you can ask other people to teach the class—that's a good way for them to learn the material, and their teaching styles might be different enough from yours that they're able to reach people whom you can't.

Weekly "Numbers" Meetings

What are the two or three numbers that measure your unit's performance week after week and month after month? What are the two or three numbers that you yourself watch to know whether you're doing a good job as a manager? Shipments? Sales? Hours billed? Performance to budget? Chances are, the key numbers that you watch relate in some way to your company's financial statements and hence ultimately affect its results. So start sharing those numbers with your team in weekly meetings. Explain where the numbers come from, why they're important, and how everybody on the team affects them. Track the trend lines over time.

You know what will happen? Pretty soon people will begin talking about the numbers themselves. They'll start figuring out ways to move the needle in the right direction. Once that begins to occur, try taking it to the next level: *forecast* where the numbers will be in the coming month or quarter. You'd be amazed how people begin to take ownership of a number once they have staked their credibility on a forecast. (We've even seen companies where employees have set up a betting pool on where a given number will be at the end of a month or quarter!)

Reinforcements: Scoreboards and Other Visual Aids

It's fashionable these days for corporate executives to have a "dashboard" on their computers, showing where the business's performance indicators stand at any given moment. We always wonder why smaller companies and operating units don't have the same thing out in the open for all employees to see. So we not only recommend discussing the key number or numbers in meetings, we also suggest posting them on a scoreboard and comparing past performance with present performance and future forecasts. When the numbers are out there for everybody to see, it's tough for people to forget or ignore them. Remember, though, that small graphs can be easily ignored—and if they can be, they will be. As with your dashboard, make sure the scoreboard is clear, straightforward, and easily visible to all.

We also like visual aids that remind people how the company makes money. They provide a context for the day-to-day focus on key numbers. Our own company has developed what we call Money Maps, illustrating topics such as where profits come from. See the sample in figure 32-1: the map traces the entire business process at a fictional company, showing how much of each sales dollar goes to paying the expenses of each department, and then highlighting how much is left over as profit. We customize them for our clients, so that everyone can see all the operations in their companies. But you can even draw maps and diagrams yourself, if you know the material well enough. A visual is always a powerful tool for reinforcing learning. When people look at it, it reminds them how they fit into the big picture. It's useful as well. One company we know of put up two copies of the same map. One showed the company's target numbers—what its best branch was doing. On the other, managers wrote their own branch's actual numbers. People could see for each critical element how close they were to, or how far away from, the best branch's performance.

FIGURE 32-1

Money Map

BUILDING FINANCIAL INTELLIGENCE IN LARGE COMPANIES

We've worked with dozens of *Fortune* 500 companies, helping them increase the level of financial intelligence in their organizations. Each of our clients seems to go about things differently, depending on its goals and its corporate culture. And of course many large companies rely on other outside trainers or create their own financial literacy programs. So we won't try to specify too much. Instead we will draw on our own experience to describe the conditions and assumptions that seem to make this kind of training work best.

Leadership Support

The whole idea of increasing people's financial intelligence is new to many large organizations, and we often encounter a significant number of skeptics or even detractors. ("Why should everyone understand finance—that's what we have an accounting organization for, isn't it?") This is why a financial training initiative is likely to require support from the top. The stronger that support, the more likely it is that people throughout the organization will buy into the idea. Companies that experience the greatest impact from financial intelligence training, typically, are those where C-suite executives believe it is essential. Those companies educate people year after year, with some individuals taking the class every year as a refresher. Some even add new classes to advance their leaders' and managers' knowledge.

Support from the top also encourages others to contribute to the initiative. When we work with a client, for instance, we customize the content of what we teach to the client's key concepts, measures, and financial results. To create that kind of program, we need help from people in various departments, but especially in finance. The financial folks are usually much happier about collaborating if they understand that the program has complete support at the top of the organization.

Assumptions and Follow-Up

One big obstacle to effective training is the assumption—common at many large companies—that people in responsible positions already know finance. A typical expression of this assumption might be, "Charlie has been a sales VP for so long, *of course* he knows how to read our financials." We know from experience that the assumption is rarely true. Many managers and executives do their jobs well enough. But because they don't truly understand financial measures and how their jobs affect those measures, they are operating well below their full potential. Think back to the twenty-one-question finance exam that we gave to a large sample of US managers. As we noted in chapter 3, the results indicated a remarkably low level of financial intelligence. So be careful not to assume that everyone understands. Assess first.

It's also difficult to get people to admit that they don't know finance. Nobody wants to look dumb in front of his or her peers, bosses, or direct reports. So there's no point in asking people to raise their hands and volunteer for a class. Instead, we almost always include the foundational elements of finance in every class—notice we call it "foundational," not "basic"—and our facilitator then assesses the needs of the group to determine where to start. Some companies require everyone to attend (so the question whether someone "needs" the training never arises); others hold classes that don't cross levels, on the assumption that participants will feel more comfortable asking questions with no bosses or direct reports in the room.

Another issue that plagues many training initiatives is a lack of follow-up. Most large companies launch new programs frequently. Most also rotate their managers through a variety of positions. So there's a danger that financial intelligence training gets lost. The best way to support ongoing financial intelligence in large organizations is to make sure that the conversation continues. Executives can talk about the numbers in meetings. If the company is public, they can ask employees to listen in on the quarterly earnings call, and then sponsor a post-call question-and-answer session. Leaders need to use every opportunity to let everyone know the importance of financial literacy.

The Practicalities

When a client asks for a training program, we naturally ask what the company wants to achieve, and what the needs of the training audience are likely to be. Then we home in on three practical questions:

- Whom do you want to attend?
- What content should we teach?
- How should we roll it out?

These discussions set the stage for successful planning and implementation of the program.

The *who* is sometimes determined in advance. For example, some clients integrate financial intelligence programs into their leadership or management development programs. But many clients start with one group, see how it goes, and then decide to roll it out to others. Some offer training at the highest level first, following up with sessions for midlevel managers and then for all employees. The logic is that the leaders can support the managers and the managers can support the rest of the organization. Others mix people from different levels in the same classes. That makes for good discussions, and it creates a feeling that everyone is in this together. The downside is that frontline employees may feel uncomfortable asking questions when their bosses are in the room with them. Still others roll out the program by function—HR first, then IT, and so on—while others simply allow open enrollment.

What to teach is obviously a critical decision, and the answer always depends on an individual company's needs. Here are some key considerations:

- *Don't assume you can skip the foundation for any audience, even leaders.* We always teach the foundational elements, just at a higher or lower level. It is a rare leader or manager who will actually tell you that he or she needs a review of these elements. By *foundation*, we mean such things as how to read an income statement and balance sheet, what revenue recognition means, and what the difference is between capitalizing and expensing.
- *Integrate your key measures and concepts.* This is an opportunity for the audience to learn what the CEO and CFO are talking about. Is free cash flow, EBITDA, or some other measure important in this industry and this company? If it is, then teach it. Review the definition, the elements, the formula, and the company's own results.
- *Determine the needs of the audience.* If you are working with salespeople, you might want to examine their customers' finances. That will help them learn how to assess customers' needs from a financial perspective. If you're working with HR people, you may want to focus on how HR has an impact on the financials (particularly since many HR people feel that they don't make an impact at all).

In all these approaches, you have to remember a few key precepts that have to do with the way adults learn. Adults learn best when the instructors combine conceptual learning with calculations using real numbers, explain the meaning of the results, and lead discussions about their impact. We bet you'll hear some amazing things, like new ideas for how to reduce downtime or improve cash flow. When people understand the big picture—and understand how what they're learning connects to their job and their impact on the company results—they'll pay close attention. Keep the teaching tightly focused, keep it fun—and remember, don't try to make anyone into an accountant!

A Final Thought: The Issue of Sharing Information

Sharing financial information makes many people nervous, and with good reason. A public company cannot share nonpublic financial data without risking violation of the rules governing insider trading. The owners of private companies may feel that nobody other than the tax authorities has a right to see the data, just as nobody has a right to peer into their personal bank accounts. Here are some thoughts about this issue, based on our experience with a large number of clients.

Public companies publish a wealth of information in their annual and quarterly reports. In our classes, most of the data we use derives directly from the annual results found in the 10-K. But we also typically ask clients to share additional information with us so that the participants can learn what they need to—measures that aren't shared publicly, for instance, or internal income statements that break down the data in helpful ways, or key concepts that are discussed internally but aren't shared externally. We keep the materials confidential, and we discuss the importance of confidentiality with the participants. Sometimes company executives worry that competitors will get the information. But financial training rarely includes material that would benefit a competitor. How is a rival likely to gain from seeing the formula a company uses for ROTC?

The issue of what to share and how to share it is actually tougher in privately held companies. Some, of course, have no problem with sharing. For those that do have concerns, we often suggest sharing the information but collecting the handouts afterward, so that there is little chance of data leaking out. Occasionally, a client decides to alter the data in ways that accurately reflect trends and ratios while not revealing the real numbers. In this case, it's important that trainees understand that the data has been camouflaged. The worst thing you can do is to make up information and pretend that it is real—it destroys trust.

Whatever your approach, don't be afraid of experimentation. There's a lot to gain from increasing the level of financial intelligence in your organization.

33

Financial Transparency: Our Ultimate Goal

FINANCIAL TRAINING IS VALUABLE, both to the people who receive it and to the company that sponsors it. But these days, even that may not go far enough.

The reason? People may not have learned a lot about finance in recent years, but they have certainly learned that they can't take their employer's financial stability for granted. Too many large companies have gone out of business or have been snapped up by an acquirer at bargain prices (usually with a huge loss of jobs). Too many companies have been shown to be cooking the books, typically with devastating consequences for the people who worked there. People all over the country have learned the lesson: for very practical reasons, they should understand something about the finances of the company they work for. Like investors, they need to know how it's doing.

So think what could be gained by a true culture of financial transparency and intelligence—a culture in which people everywhere actually saw and learned to understand the financial statements. No, we don't expect everyone to become Wall Street analysts or accountants. We just think that if the financials are out there and the key concepts repeatedly explained, every employee in the place will be more trusting and more loyal, and the company will be stronger for it. To be sure, publicly traded companies can't show consolidated financials to employees except once a quarter, when the information is released to the public. But they can certainly make a point of explaining those financials when they are released. In the meantime, they can make sure that employees see operating numbers for the department or facility they work in.

You can see that we believe passionately in the power of knowledge—and when it comes to business, we believe most of all in the power of financial knowledge and the financial intelligence necessary to put it to work. Financial information is the nervous system of any business. It contains the data that show how the business is faring—where its strengths are, where its weaknesses are, where its opportunities and threats are as well. For too long, a relative handful of people in each company are the only ones who have understood what the financial data was telling them. We think more people should understand it—starting with managers but ultimately extending out into the entire workforce. People will be better off for gaining that understanding, and so will companies.

Part 8
Toolbox

UNDERSTANDING SARBANES-OXLEY

If you are anywhere near your finance department, you have heard of Sarbanes-Oxley, also known as Sarbox or just Sox. Sarbanes-Oxley is a law enacted by the US Congress in July 2002 in response to continuing revelations of financial fraud. It may be the most significant legislation affecting corporate governance, financial disclosure, and public accounting since the original US securities laws were enacted in the 1930s. It is designed to improve the public's confidence in the financial markets by strengthening financial reporting controls and the penalties for noncompliance.

Sarbanes-Oxley's provisions affect nearly everyone involved with finance (and most of the operations folks, too). The law created the Public Company Accounting Oversight Board. It bans accounting firms from selling both audit and nonaudit services to clients. It requires corporate boards of directors to include at least one director who is a financial expert and requires board audit committees to establish procedures whereby employees can confidentially tip off directors to fraudulent accounting. Under Sarbanes-Oxley, a company cannot fire, demote, or harass employees who attempt to report suspected financial fraud.

CEOs and CFOs are greatly affected by the law. These officers must certify their company's quarterly and annual financial statements, attest that they are responsible for disclosure and control procedures, and affirm that the financial statements don't contain misrepresentations. Most companies we work with now have extensive approval and sign-off procedures each quarter. Since the CEO and CFO are on the hook for the financials, they often want every division president to sign for his or her division. Indeed, signoffs may extend several levels down. According to the law, fines and jail time may be required if financial results are misrepresented intentionally. Also, the law forbids companies from granting or guaranteeing personal loans to executives and directors. (A study by the nonprofit Corporate Library Research Group found that companies lent executives more than $4.5 billion in 2001, just prior to the law's enactment, often at no or low interest.) And it requires CEOs or CFOs to give back certain bonuses and stock option profits if their company is forced to restate financial results because of misconduct.

Sarbanes-Oxley requires companies to strengthen their internal controls. They must include an "internal controls report" in their annual report to shareholders, addressing management's responsibility in maintaining adequate controls over financial reporting and stating a conclusion as to the effectiveness of the controls. In addition, management must disclose information on material changes in the financial condition or operations of the company on a rapid and current basis.

Sarbanes-Oxley forces public companies to take more responsibility for their financial statements, and may lessen the probability of undetected fraud. However, it is very expensive to implement. The average cost for companies is $5 million; for large companies such as General Electric, it may be as much as $30 million.

APPENDIX

Sample Financials

The following is a sample set of financials for an imaginary company.

SAMPLE INCOME STATEMENT

(in millions)

	Year ending December 31, 2012
Sales	$8,689
Cost of goods sold	6,756
Gross profit	**$1,933**
Selling, general, and admin. (SG&A)	$1,061
Depreciation	239
Other income	19
EBIT	**$ 652**
Interest expense	191
Taxes	213
Net profit	**$ 248**

SAMPLE BALANCE SHEET

(in millions)

	12/31/2012	12/31/2011
Assets		
Cash and cash equivalents	$ 83	$ 72
Accounts receivable	1,312	1,204
Inventory	1,270	1,514
Other current assets and accruals	85	67
Total current assets	2,750	2,857
Property, plant, and equipment	2,230	2,264
Other long-term assets	213	233
Total assets	**$5,193**	**$5,354**
Liabilities		
Accounts payable	$1,022	$1,129
Credit line	100	150
Current portion of long-term debt	52	51
Total current liabilities	1,174	1,330
Long-term debt	1,037	1,158
Other long-term liabilities	525	491
Total liabilities	**$2,736**	**$2,979**
Shareholders' equity		
Common stock, $1 par value (100,000,000 authorized, 74,000,000 outstanding in 2012 and 2011)	$ 74	$ 74
Additional paid-in capital	1,110	1,110
Retained earnings	1,273	1,191
Total shareholders' equity	**$2,457**	**$2,375**
Total liabilities and shareholders' equity	**$5,193**	**$5,354**

2012 footnotes:

Depreciation	*$239*
Number of common shares (mil)	*74*
Earnings per share	*$3.35*
Dividend per share	*$2.24*

SAMPLE CASH FLOW STATEMENT

(in millions)

	Year ending December 31, 2012
Cash from operating activities	
Net profit	$ 248
Depreciation	239
Accounts receivable	(108)
Inventory	244
Other current assets	(18)
Accounts payable	(107)
Cash from operations	**$ 498**
Cash from investing activities	
Property, plant, and equipment	$ (205)
Other long-term assets	20
Cash from investing	**$ (185)**
Cash from financing activities	
Credit line	$ (50)
Current portion of long-term debt	1
Long-term debt	(121)
Other long-term liabilities	34
Equity	(166)
Cash from financing	**$ (302)**
Change in cash	11
Cash at beginning	72
Cash at end	**$ 83**

NOTES

Chapter 1

1. Deloitte Forensic Center, *Ten Things About Financial Statement Fraud: A Review of SEC Enforcement Releases, 2000–2006* (June 2007), http://www.deloitte.com/view/en_US/us/Services/Financial-Advisory-Services/Forensic-Center/5ac81266d7115210VgnVCM100000ba42f00aRCRD.htm.

Chapter 3

1. For more, see our article, "Are Your People Financially Literate?" *Harvard Business Review*, October 2009, 28.

2. Mike France, "Why Bernie Before Kenny-Boy?" *BusinessWeek*, March 15, 2004, 37.

Chapter 4

1. Michael Rapoport, "U.S. Firms Clash Over Accounting Rules," *Wall Street Journal*, July 6, 2011.

Chapter 6

1. H. Thomas Johnson and Robert S. Kaplan, *Relevance Lost: The Rise and Fall of Management Accounting* (Boston: Harvard Business School Press, 1991).

Chapter 7

1. See "Vitesse Semiconductor Announces Results of the Review by the Special Committee of the Board," *Business Wire*, December 19, 2006; U.S. Securities and Exchange Commission, Litigation Release No. 21769, December 10, 2010; and Accounting and Auditing Enforcement Release No. 3217, December 10, 2010, "SEC Charges Vitesse Semiconductor Corporation and Four Former Vitesse Executives in Revenue Recognition and Options Backdating Schemes."

Chapter 8

1. Randall Smith and Steven Lipin, "Odd Numbers: Are Companies Using Restructuring Costs to Fudge the Figures?" *Wall Street Journal*, January 30, 1996.

Chapter 9

1. For a brief summary, see Kathleen Day, "Study Finds 'Extensive' Fraud at Fannie Mae," *Washington Post*, May 24, 2006.

Chapter 11

1. Manjeet Kripalani, "India's Madoff? Satyam Scandal Rocks Outsourcing Industry," *Bloomberg Business Week*, January 7, 2009.

Chapter 25

1. Bo Burlingham, *Small Giants: Companies That Choose to Be Great Instead of Big* (New York: Portfolio, 2007).

2. See Chris Zook and James Allen, *Repeatability: Build Enduring Businesses for a World of Constant Change* (Boston: Harvard Business Review Press, 2012).

Chapter 31

1. U.S. Marine Corps Staff, *Warfighting* (New York: Crown Business, 1995).

2. Edward E. Lawler, Susan A. Mohrman, and Gerald E. Ledford, "Creating High Performance Organizations" (Los Angeles: Center for Effective Organizations, Marshall School of Business, University of Southern California, 1995).

ACKNOWLEDGMENTS

We—Karen and Joe—have been working together for more than twelve years. Our partnership began with a chance meeting at a conference and evolved over time into co-ownership of our company, the Business Literacy Institute, and now into coauthorship of this book. Over the years, we have met, worked with, and shared experiences with many people who have had an impact on our thinking and our work. This book is a culmination of our education, of our work and management experiences, of our research, of our partnership, and of all we have learned from our work with thousands of employees, managers, and leaders.

Karen first met John while conducting research for her dissertation. He was, and still is, one of the preeminent experts on open-book management and a highly respected business author. We kept track of each other through the years and were always interested in each other's work. Karen was delighted when John wanted to be a part of this project. He has been an indispensable part of the team.

Many other people have helped make this book a reality. Among them:

- The readers of the first edition of *Financial Intelligence*. We knew when we wrote the first book that there was a need for a down-to-earth, real-world book about finance. But we had no idea we were writing a best-seller! This second edition is available in part because so many of these readers recommended the book, shared it, and bought it for people they knew would benefit from it.

- Bo Burlingham, an editor-at-large at *Inc.* magazine, author of the wonderful book *Small Giants*, and coauthor (with Jack Stack) of *The Great Game of Business* and *A Stake in the Outcome*. Bo graciously shared with us the research and writing on financial fraud that he and Joe had gathered for another project.

- Joe Cornwell and Joe VanDenBerghe, founders of Setpoint (at Setpoint they were referred to simply as "the Joes"). We're grateful for their belief in teaching everyone the financials and for their tireless efforts in encouraging everyone at Setpoint to participate actively in the success of the company. We also want to thank Setpoint's current CEO, Brad Angus, who has been extremely helpful as an adviser to this second edition. We're glad they let us tell some Setpoint stories. We also want to acknowledge Reid Leland (owner of LeanWerks), Mark Coy, Machel Jackson, Jason Munns, Steve Neutzman, Kara Smith, Roger Thomas, and all the Setpoint employees for helping us refine our approach to financial intelligence. If you are ever in Utah, you should visit Setpoint; the company's system works, and you'll see both financial intelligence and psychic ownership in action. We suspect you'll be surprised at employees' depth of understanding of the business and their commitment to its success.

- Our clients at the Business Literacy Institute. Thanks to their commitment to financial literacy, we have been able to help spread financial intelligence throughout many organizations. It's impossible to thank them all, but a few who cheered us on during the writing of this second edition are Heidi Flaherty and the team at Advent; the Association of General Contractors; Cheryl Mackie at CVS Caremark; Andy Billings at Electronic Arts; Jeff Detrick, Michael Guarnieri, Ellie Murphy, and the entire team at General Electric; Valorie McClelland and Ginny Hoverman at Goodrich; Jim Roberts, Tom Case, Ron Gatto, Catherine Hambley and the team at Granite Construction; Tiffany Keller at Gulfstream, Tanya Chermack at Harvard Vanguard; the Independent College Bookstore Association; Becky Nawrocki at the Institute of Supply Management; Gayle Tomlinson at Kraton; Michael Sigmund at MacDermid Incorporated; Michelle Duke and Anne Frenette at the National Association of Broadcasters; Steve Capas, David Pietrycha, Christy Shibata, Mary von Herrmann, and the teams at NBC News and NBC Universal; Manu Varma at Sierra Wireless; the Society of Human Resource Management; Meghan O'Leary and Stacy Pell at Silicon Valley Bank; Beth Goldstein at Smile Brands; Melinda Del Toro and Ron Wangerin at Viasat; and Mariela Saravia at Visa.

- Our colleagues at the Business Literacy Institute. Our facilitation team—Jim Bado, Cathy Ivancic, Hovig Tchalian, and Ed Westfield—are all top-notch trainers, with their own unique styles that make taking a class from them an enriching experience. Stephanie Wexler is manager of client services; her professionalism keeps our projects on track. Judy Golove, manager of training development, ensures that all our training programs are of the highest quality. Kara Smith also works in training development, joining Judy in keeping our programs top notch. Sharon Maas's extensive knowledge of business literacy is reflected in our customized training program content. Brad Angus, our business development manager, works tirelessly to ensure we are meeting our clients' needs. Kathy Hoye is the team's administrative assistant, keeping everything running smoothly.

- Dave Merrill, the creative artist who illustrates our Money Maps. His ability to take our initial rough ideas and bring them to life is a true talent.
- Jonathan Troper and the team at Alliant International University's Marshall Goldsmith School of Management, who worked with us to conduct the national study in which we assessed the financial intelligence of US managers and leaders. We relied on their expertise to ensure that the financial intelligence test itself and our approach were statistically valid and reliable, giving us accurate data about where US managers and leaders stand in terms of their financial intelligence.
- Our agent, James Levine.
- Tim Sullivan, our editor; and the rest of the team at Harvard Business Review Press, with a special thank you to Julie Devoll.
- And all the others who have helped us along the way, including Helen and Gene Berman, Tony Bonenfant, Kelin Gersick, Larry and Jewel Knight, Nellie Lal, Michael Lee and the Main Graphics team, Don Mankin, Philomena McAndrew, Alen Miller, Loren Roberts, Marlin Shelley, Brian Shore, Roberta Wolff, Paige Woodward, Joanne Worrell, and Brian Zander. Our heartfelt thanks to all.

INDEX

ABOUT THE AUTHORS

Karen Berman, PhD, is founder and co-owner of the Business Literacy Institute, a consulting firm offering customized financial intelligence training programs, financial intelligence assessments, Money Maps, and other products and services designed to ensure that everyone in organizations understands how financial success is measured and how they make an impact. Karen has worked with dozens of *Fortune* 100 companies, helping them to create financial literacy programs that transform employees, managers, and leaders into business partners.

Joe Knight is co-owner of the Business Literacy Institute and a principal owner of Setpoint Companies, where he is also chief financial officer. He is a senior facilitator and keynote speaker for the Business Literacy Institute, traveling to clients and conferences all over the world to teach them about finance. Joe is a true believer in financial transparency and lives it every day at Setpoint.